"We are called to go from glory to gl[...]
stewards with the gifts and callings that the Holy Spirit bestows
upon us. Is it possible to grow in grace? What does it look like
to step out in faith? Are there new horizons for us to venture
into even if you are a veteran in ministry? Jennifer LeClaire
declares an unequivocal *Yes!* Yes, we are to continuously 'come
up higher' and graduate into new levels of gifting, wisdom and
character. If you need a challenge to spur you on, then *Becoming
a Next-Level Prophet* is written with you in mind."

Dr. James W. Goll, founder, God Encounters Ministries
and GOLL Ideation; author, speaker, recording artist
and communications trainer

"Thank God for the new generation of prophets like Jennifer
LeClaire that God is bringing forth at this time. I pioneered the
prophetic movement in 1988, but we are now in the second phase
of prophets and the prophetic ministry fulfilling God's end time
purpose for Christ's Church and God's Word to the nations."

Bishop Bill Hamon, Christian International Apostolic
and Global Networks; author, *The Eternal Church*,
Prophets and the Prophetic Movement,
God's Weapons of War and more

"*Becoming a Next-Level Prophet* by Jennifer LeClaire is an
insightful key for the new generation of prophetic voices to
step into what God is doing on the earth in this season. With
biblical illustrations, personal stories and powerful activations,
Jennifer leads the reader into the depths of God's heart for
prophecy, for His prophets and for the Body of Christ! I highly
recommend this book!"

Kris Vallotton, senior associate leader, Bethel Church,
Redding, California; co-founder, Bethel School of
Supernatural Ministry; author, including *The Supernatural
Ways of Royalty*, *Heavy Rain* and *Poverty, Riches and Wealth*

BECOMING
A NEXT-LEVEL
PROPHET

BECOMING
A NEXT-LEVEL
PROPHET

AN INVITATION **TO INCREASE** IN YOUR GIFT

JENNIFER LeCLAIRE

Chosen

a division of Baker Publishing Group
Minneapolis, Minnesota

© 2019 by Revelation Media Networks

Published by Chosen Books
Minneapolis, Minnesota
www.chosenbooks.com

Chosen Books is a division of
Baker Publishing Group, Grand Rapids, Michigan

Printed in the United States of America

Library of Congress Cataloging-in-Publication Data
Names: LeClaire, Jennifer (Jennifer L.), author.
Title: Becoming a next-level prophet : an invitation to increase in your gift / Jennifer LeClaire.
Description: Minneapolis : Chosen, a division of Baker Publishing Group, 2019.
Identifiers: LCCN 2018053590 | ISBN 9780800799359 (trade paper : alk. paper) | ISBN 9781493418886 (e-book)
Subjects: LCSH: Prophecy—Christianity. | Gifts, Spiritual.
Classification: LCC BR115.P8 L425 2019 | DDC 234/.13—dc23
LC record available at https://lccn.loc.gov/2018053590

I dedicate this book to the new generation of prophets that is rising—a generation that is pursuing His love more than man's recognition, a generation that is cultivating a passion for Jesus rather than fulfilling the passions of the flesh, a generation that refuses to compromise with a world that is pressing for tolerance of what God calls evil. I believe this new generation of prophetic voices can help lead the Church into repentance and pave the way for the greatest Great Awakening the world has ever seen.

Contents

Foreword

The Bible so fixates us on the role of the prophetic and prophets that they end up being the most important, sought-after people in their day in the Old Testament. In the New Testament their role is just as unique and important, and they are not only highlighted but featured many times in title, story and theology. As a matter of fact, Paul emphasizes the gift of prophecy as the most important of all spiritual gifts in 1 Corinthians 14:1 because it helps us to connect most quickly to the love of God and because we get to hear His heart, process and intention for ourselves or the world around us.

When prophets emerge in society, they function much like who Jesus said the Holy Spirit will be to us: They are comforters, counselors, friends who help become navigation systems to humanity. They are people God speaks through, because God loves the world so much He sends His friends to speak into the heart of it. Time with a prophet may save someone therapy sessions, life-coaching times or even time with a master business coach or strategist in your industry. Prophets help bring spiritual clarity and direction and help us to bypass what is considered normal.

God is restoring the dignity of the office of a prophet and these amazing revelation gifts. People are becoming aware of what prophets can bring to the world, and this is causing a spiritual hunger to hear God's voice like never before. When prophets made an appearance in the Bible, they were never people who just heard from God for the sake of hearing information. They were not just gifted people either. They were the friends of God who understood His perceptions about reality and could relate His divine will and heart, not just information. I believe this generation is becoming aware again that there are prophets among us.

As you read this book by Jennifer, you are going to see the function, authority and role of the prophetic in this hour. One of my favorite lines as she defines the process is that "Prophets may be called from their mother's womb, but they are not born overnight." I have longed for practical tools about such significant topics such as prophets, and this is one of those very practical guides, but it is so profound because it imparts the spiritual culture that keeps someone in their lane as a prophet.

In some ways the role of a prophet is one of the most sacrificial of all the major roles you can take on in public or relational ministry. Prophets are the ultimate servants, giving without expecting a return on earth, but getting fed like Jesus with food that many people do not even consider: friendship with God. Because so little has been defined about the prophetic office, the road to it has been hard for many to navigate; this book will help keep the checks and balances of right thinking, good character practices and healthy process in front of you. Not only does it impart the principles, but then Jennifer takes you through practical steps to pray through, ponder and define for your own life about your own calling, lifestyle and practice. In some ways as I was reading it, I felt it was a discipleship manual for anyone who wants to carry the authority of Christ. She does a thorough job of taking you through a step-by-step process of applying what it takes to walk into the level of anointing that will actually fulfill the hunger you have to experience God.

Ultimately that is it, though, right? God puts in us this incredible calling—a deep hunger for significance in walking with Him, spiritual gifts—and then we go on a journey to really manifest the greatness of what He has put inside us. As a prophet, there is this period between when you are walking in your Promised Land or in fullness and when you are learning who God is, who you are and how to love the people He has called you to. Jennifer helps to accelerate that process, and you will find yourself going to the next level so you can bring the world around you to the next level if you follow her example and writings.

Shawn Bolz, www.bolzministries.com,
author, *Translating God, Modern Prophets* and *God Secrets*;
host, *Exploring the Prophetic* podcast and *Translating God* on TBN

Acknowledgments

I appreciate the pioneers of the modern-day prophetic movement who have taught me so much over the last decades. Many thanks to Jane Campbell and the Chosen team for being on the cutting edge of publishing prophetic materials that cross gaps into mainstream Christianity. I am grateful for my Awakening House of Prayer team, who continue to support me through the warfare that accompanies writing.

Introduction

Do you want to get to the next level in your prophetic gifting? If your objective is to become a more accurate mouthpiece for God, to be more sensitive to His Spirit, to pray more effectively and to point more people to Jesus, then God is well pleased. Your motives qualify you to come up higher—and move deeper—in prophetic ministry.

I penned these pages for those who are not the sort of seers seeking fame and fortune. I wrote these words for those who are not the manner of mouthpiece who wants to make a spectacle of your spiritual gifts or the variety of prophet who vies for preaching invitations on the ministry circuit. I offer these revelations to those who just want to be good stewards of the gifts with which God has entrusted them.

Before you set your heart to progress in the prophetic, check your motives. The last thing you want to do is run your race for the wrong prize. The prize is not recognition. The prize is not money. The prize is not earthly. The prize is eternal. There is a price to pay to attain the prize, and only those willing to pay it will progress down the road to eternal reward.

Now, the only question is this: Are you willing to pay that price for progress? Wait; do not answer too quickly.

In his classic book *Mere Christianity*, C. S. Lewis wrote:

> Progress means getting nearer to the place where you want to be. And if you have taken a wrong turning, then to go forward does not get you any nearer. If you are on the wrong road, progress means doing an about-turn and walking back to the right road; and in that case the man who turns back soonest is the most progressive man.[1]

Like Lewis said, if you are on the wrong road—if you have a skewed idea of the purpose of prophetic ministry and the lifestyle of a prophet—then turn back. Repent and seek God's heart for the ministry He has given you and take the time to cultivate the character required to fulfill your call so you do not have to make a U-turn one hundred miles down the highway.

So again, are you willing to pay the price for progress? Wait; do not answer too quickly.

Let me first share with you some of the costs. Although I deal with this topic extensively in my book *The Making of a Prophet: Practical Advice for Developing Your Prophetic Voice* (Chosen, 2014), I will give you something to consider immediately: You will have to let go of some things—perhaps even some people— that are weighing you down. The painful reality is that you cannot always hold onto what you have and go where God ultimately wants you to go. In fact, you may have to set out on a journey with God in blind faith, not knowing where He is taking you or what you will find there. The prophet Abram had to do both.

God told Abram to leave his country, his family and his father's home for a land He would show him. It was a drastic command, but there was a drastic promise attached to it:

> I will make of you a great nation; I will bless you and make your name great, so that you will be a blessing. I will bless them who bless you and curse him who curses you, and in you all families of the earth will be blessed.
>
> Genesis 12:2–3

Abram could not enter into the fullness of a prophetic covenant with God without leaving some old associations behind. Now, this radical move probably did not make any sense to Abram's family and friends. I am certain the prophet's choice was not honored among the people living in his Babylonian hometown of Ur, where people served false gods. I imagine he, like Noah, was mocked for following the voice of a God he could not see out of a then-modern city and into the wilderness. It probably did not even make much sense to Abram. But something in Abram knew that the promise was worth the price he had to pay. Abram did not fully understand it at the time, but Jehovah was calling him as a prophet, and he answered.

If you want to rise to the next level in the prophetic, you need to determine in your heart right now to set your face like flint and refuse to give up. Believe me, you will feel like giving up more often than you will want to admit. I have offered God my resignation letter on more than one occasion. He never accepts it. One time He told me, "I'm impressed at how you press through the pressure." The pressure is real and sometimes so intense that I find myself considering David's cry:

> Give ear to my prayer, O God, and do not hide Yourself from my supplication. Attend to me, and answer me; I am restless in my complaint, and I murmur, because of the voice of the enemy, because of the pressure of the wicked, for they cause trouble to drop on me, and in wrath they have animosity against me.
>
> My heart is in pain within me, and the terrors of death have fallen on me. Fear and trembling come into me, and horror has overwhelmed me. I said, "Oh, that I had wings like a dove! For then I would fly away and be at rest. Indeed, then I would wander far off, and remain in the wilderness. Selah I would hasten my escape from the windy storm and tempest."
>
> Psalm 55:1–8

The hard truth is God sometimes uses trials and tribulations to set the stage for our next level, because trials and tribulations make us more desperate to hear His voice and more willing to follow His Spirit. I am not saying He is the one who brings the trials and tribulations, though sometimes He will drive us into the wilderness, where we have to face our flesh and then overcome the enemy's temptations by standing on His Word. The Holy Spirit led Jesus, our prototype Prophet, into the wilderness. There He was tempted by the devil after forty days and forty nights of fasting (see Matthew 4:1–11). Jesus had to stay true to the Word of God during this trial to fulfill His ministry.

Beyond the wilderness, Jesus was later tempted to abort His ministry a second time. You remember the scene in the Garden of Gethsemane. Jesus was praying while His best friends slept a few feet away instead of making intercession for Him. Indeed, the trial was so fierce His sweat actually became like great drops of blood (see Luke 22:44). I do not know about you, but I have not yet resisted to the point of bloodshed while striving against sin (see Hebrews 12:4).

The next-level ascension process is not for the faint of heart. If you want to climb to higher heights in prophetic ministry, you will be met with resistance from the enemy, resistance from people and resistance from your flesh. But know this: If you do not give up—if you keep pressing through the pressure—you will make progress toward perfection (maturation). You might not see it in your day-to-day walk with God, but the fruit will manifest, and it will glorify Him.

Now that you have considered some of the costs, consider the other side of the blade. Like a dull knife, a dull prophetic edge is dangerous. Cooking experts attest that it takes more force to cut through food with a dull knife because you have to apply more pressure, and that makes losing control of the knife more likely. A dull knife tends to slip on the surface of the object you are slicing. The result is often a painful injury.

True prophets and prophetic people need to sharpen their prophetic edge regularly so they do not cause a painful injury to those to whom they are ministering with inaccurate utterances. True prophetic words, like the written Word of God, are sharp.

> For the word of God is alive, and active, and sharper than any two-edged sword, piercing even to the division of soul and spirit, of joints and marrow, and able to judge the thoughts and intents of the heart. There is no creature that is not revealed in His sight, for all things are bare and exposed to the eyes of Him to whom we must give account.
>
> Hebrews 4:12–13

Are you ready to find out exactly how to sharpen your prophetic edge, cut your way through resistance and ascend to the next level? Although training seminars—the world's equivalent to continuing education for professionals like doctors and lawyers—are worth the investment, moving into your next level is not merely about more training seminars. To be sure, it is more about your response to God, people, circumstances and your own flesh. I pray that as you read the words on these pages the Holy Spirit will show you the areas of your soul He is ready to work on so you can cooperate with the grace of God. Let's get started.

1

Your Prophetic Gifting

Also I heard the voice of the Lord saying, "Whom
shall I send, and who will go for us?" Then I said,
"Here am I. Send me."

Isaiah 6:8

Although the same Lord Himself calls all prophets, all prophetic giftings are somewhat unique because every prophet's
mission is unique. Exploring your prophetic calling can help
you understand your prophetic mission and what it will take
to prepare for and progress through each level on your way to
fulfilling your God-given destiny.

The apostle Paul outlines the who, what, when, where and
why of the prophetic ministry in Ephesians 4:11–13 (NLT):

Now these are the gifts Christ gave to the church: the apostles,
the prophets, the evangelists, and the pastors and teachers.
Their responsibility is to equip God's people to do his work
and build up the church, the body of Christ. This will continue
until we all come to such unity in our faith and knowledge of
God's Son that we will be mature in the Lord, measuring up to
the full and complete standard of Christ.

23

So we see that Jesus gives ascension gift prophets to the Church for a critical function: to equip God's people to do His work and build up the Church.

The Contemporary English Version says, "Christ chose some of us to be apostles, prophets, missionaries, pastors, and teachers, so that his people would learn to serve and his body would grow strong" (Ephesians 4:11–12). I like the CEV translation because it brings the prophetic ministry to the modern day. Prophets are just as critical today as they ever were. That is why Christ is still choosing some Christians to be apostles, prophets, evangelists, pastors and teachers.

It is not a calling for the elite. It is a call to dedicated, lifelong service to the Body of Christ. And, as I mentioned in the introduction, there is a price to pay.

New Testament prophets are also called to edify, comfort and exhort (see 1 Corinthians 14:3). Prophets are called to stand in the gap and make up a hedge (see Ezekiel 22:30). Prophets have a heart-turning ministry—to turn the hearts of the fathers toward the children and the hearts of the children toward the fathers (see Malachi 4:6). Prophets are reformers. Prophets prepare a way for the Lord (see John 1:23) and separate the profane from the holy (see Ezekiel 44:23).[1]

With all this in mind, let's look at the calling, commissionings and missions of some prophets in the Bible. God chronicled the details of their callings on purpose. These callings and commissionings will show us that prophetic ministry manifests through different prophets in different ways. Though the foundation for prophetic ministry remains unchanged, God uses prophets in different roles at different times for different purposes.

Do Not Get Ahead of God

Moses offers a sobering lesson for emerging prophets: Do not get ahead of God. Moses accurately sensed God's calling on his life as a deliverer, but he stepped into his ministry in the wrong timing and in the wrong way. He had the purpose and the passion, but he lacked the spiritual maturity and wisdom to lead the Israelites out of Egypt.

Here is a quick overview: Moses grew up in Pharaoh's household. When he came of age, he was grieved at how his people, the Hebrews, were toiling and laboring so hard for so little. When he saw an Egyptian beating a Hebrew, his passion boiled up on the inside of him, and he took matters into his own hands by murdering the Egyptian (see Exodus 2:12). That was not God's will or God's way. Moses demonstrated he was not yet ready for God's high calling. He had a prophetic edge, but it was dull.

I see this happen a lot in today's prophetic ministry circles. Young believers—or even sometimes mature believers—stand in a prayer line while a visiting apostle or prophet boldly declares a prophetic calling in front of the congregation. Excited by this prophetic calling, these believers rush ahead of the commissioning of God and the wisdom of God and try to operate in gifts that are not yet fully developed without any training or supervision. Notice I said *try*. They, like Moses, may have a prophetic edge, but it is dull. It has been identified and activated, but it has not been sharpened.

When immature prophets race out into the ministry field without equipping or accountability, there is strong potential for twofold harm. First, the unseasoned prophet often prophesies inaccurate, soulish, incomplete or untimely words to hungry saints who are desperately seeking God's true direction for their lives. Some may be led astray by those utterances.

Second, the unseasoned prophet can step into a land mine of accusations over his or her ministry that can take a lasting toll on a true gifting. Indeed, too many unseasoned prophets have been labeled false prophets because they were not sent; they just went with admirable zeal and giftings they did not understand how to steward. Unfortunately, even a pure heart can do a lot of damage to the prophetic ministry at large.

Now back to Moses. Moses murdered an Egyptian to defend his Hebrew brother, but the Israelites did not seem to appreciate the deliverance. In fact, one of them asked, "Who made you a prince and a judge over us?" (Exodus 2:14). God did, actually. God had Moses in mind as a ruler and judge over the Israelites. Moses sensed that burden in his heart, but he got ahead of God's commissioning. The result: He had to hide on the back side of the desert for forty years before he would reemerge into his prophetic purpose. It was during this time that God prepared him to rise up as a deliverer.

Maybe you sense a prophetic calling on your life, but no one else recognizes it. Just be patient and ask the Holy Spirit to train you in the prophetic. Invest in prophetic training resources from reputable, proven ministries and, like Paul told Timothy, study to show yourself approved (see 2 Timothy 2:15). Begin to operate in some of the fundamentals of prophetic ministry, like prayer and intercession. Consecrate yourself to the Lord and commit to dying to self. In other words, feed the gift. Work with the Holy Spirit to prepare your heart. But do not get ahead of God, because that will only delay your destiny.

Moses' Calling to Be a Deliverer

After Moses fled to the desert in fear (see Exodus 2:15), he seemed to forget all about Israel. He got married, had children and tended his father-in-law Jethro's sheep. Then, suddenly—have you ever experienced one of God's suddenlies?—Jehovah came on the scene with one of the most unique callings we see in Scripture. Let's read from Exodus 3:2–3:

> The angel of the LORD appeared to him in a flame of fire from the midst of a bush, and he looked, and the bush burned with

fire, but the bush was not consumed. So Moses said, "I will now turn aside and see this great sight, why the bush is not burnt."

This was a test. Moses could have continued heading back to the west side of the wilderness. But he was spiritually sensitive enough to take notice of the strange sight.

I remember one time I was coming into my condo and I saw a smoking bush. It was the strangest thing. Following in Moses' footsteps, I went to examine the matter. I was not taking any chances on missing the Lord. As it was with Moses, the Lord saw that I took notice of the strange sight and spoke an important message to my heart. What about you? Do you have spiritual eyes to see and spiritual ears to hear God in any circumstance? I am not saying God is talking through every strange happening. What I am saying is that we need to be spiritually in tune so we can perceive Him when He is talking.

My point is this: God can talk to you anytime, anywhere, through anything. Keep your spiritual eyes and ears on, and of course test all things and hold fast to that which is good (see 1 Thessalonians 5:21).

Let's continue reading the account, picking up at Exodus 3:4–10:

> When the LORD saw that he turned aside to see, God called to him from out of the midst of the bush and said, "Moses, Moses."
>
> And he said, "Here am I."
>
> He said, "Do not approach here. Remove your sandals from off your feet, for the place on which you are standing is holy ground." Moreover He said, "I am the God of your father, the God of Abraham, the God of Isaac, and the God of Jacob." And Moses hid his face, for he was afraid to look upon God.
>
> The LORD said, "I have surely seen the affliction of My people who are in Egypt and have heard their cry on account of their taskmasters, for I know their sorrows. Therefore, I have come

down to deliver them out of the hand of the Egyptians, and to bring them up out of that land to a good and spacious land, to a land flowing with milk and honey, to the place of the Canaanites, the Hittites, the Amorites, the Perizzites, the Hivites, and the Jebusites. Now therefore, the cry of the children of Israel has come to Me. Moreover, I have also seen the oppression with which the Egyptians are oppressing them. Come now therefore, and I will send you to Pharaoh so that you may bring forth My people, the children of Israel, out of Egypt."

What a calling! Talk about exceedingly abundantly more than you can ask or think. Now, after this supernatural encounter with God, Moses did not puff up in pride and try to book meetings with Pharaoh to vindicate himself with the Hebrews in Egypt. While Moses got out ahead of God forty years earlier, this time Moses argued with God over his own ability to answer the call and fulfill the mission. Verse 11 tells us, "Moses said to God, 'Who am I that I should go to Pharaoh and that I should bring forth the children of Israel out of Egypt?'" In fact, most of God's prophets responded to God's call with similar feelings of unworthiness or fear. This is a proper reaction, in my opinion, because it demonstrates their humility before the Lord and their awesome calling, which is not to be taken lightly. The Bible says that Moses was the meekest man on the face of the earth (see Numbers 12:3). That should be the prophet's reputation.

This is also noteworthy: In Moses' case, the calling and the commissioning took place at the same time. It does not always happen that way, and I will venture to say that it does not usually happen that way. In other words, when God calls prophets today, they do not usually step onto a national scene and stand before pharaohs (or presidents, kings, prime ministers or other dignitaries) with prophetic words from God immediately. After the calling there is usually a season of preparation followed by a commissioning to a smaller assignment before God takes the prophet to the next level.

Samuel Speaks into Government

Samuel was called as a young boy. We know the boy Samuel ministered before the Lord under the authority of the priest Eli. In those days the prophetic word of the Lord was rare (see 1 Samuel 3:1). There were not many visions.

One night, young Samuel was lying in the temple, minding his own business, and the Lord called him. You know the story. Samuel did not immediately recognize the call. The Bible says he "did not yet know the LORD" (1 Samuel 3:7). How many of us are like that? God is calling us to do something, and we respond inappropriately—or we do not respond at all—because we just are not sure it was really God. Our hearts are right, but it takes us longer to get in line with God's will because we are unfamiliar with the way the Lord is moving or speaking. We do not yet know the Lord in that way.

Eli did know the ways of the Lord. So the third time Samuel came running in obedience to what he thought was Eli's beckoning, the old, dim-eyed priest caught on to what was happening and told the boy what to do. Thank God that in our ignorance His mercy continues to reach out to us. When God called Samuel a fourth time he followed Eli's instructions and responded, "Speak, for Your servant listens" (verse 10). Then the Lord told young Samuel some disturbing news about judgment coming upon Eli's family that may have made him wish he had rolled over and plugged his ears.

I can relate. When the Lord first called me into prophetic ministry I received lots of warnings about enemy assignments coming down the pike. I had dreams of the plots and plans of murderous religious spirits. I did not want to release these prophetic communications, and nobody really wanted to hear them. Thankfully, I was surrounded by more mature prophetic voices who were able to help me process what I was hearing, learn how to pray it through and discern when, how and with whom to share the Spirit-inspired warnings.

Samuel did not have that luxury. The next morning, Eli asked Samuel what the Lord had said. The Bible says he was scared to tell Eli (verse 15). This was Samuel's test. Would he fear man more than he trusted God? Samuel passed the test and in doing so sharpened his prophetic edge. Indeed, young Samuel seemed to rise in his prophetic anointing and stature rapidly. The Bible says the Lord was with Samuel as he grew up, and He let none "of his words fall to the ground" (verse 19). All Israel from Dan to Beersheba recognized that Samuel was a prophet of the Lord.

Samuel's mission dealt with leadership in God's Kingdom. Again, his first prophetic utterance was a judgment on the house of Eli (see verses 11–14). Samuel eventually became judge in Eli's place; he served in this role until the Israelites demanded a king so they could be like other nations.

Samuel continued moving in a governmental anointing. It was Samuel who anointed Israel's first king, Saul (see 1 Samuel 10:1). It was Samuel who mentored him. It was Samuel too who rebuked him for his disobedience to God (see 1 Samuel 13). When God grew weary of Saul's disobedience, He sent Samuel to anoint a new king, David (see 1 Samuel 16). Samuel also launched a school of the prophets to raise up the next generation of prophetic leaders (see 1 Samuel 10:5). Dealing with leadership issues, then, was a main part of Samuel's mission, and it was so from the first time God spoke to him.

Watchman Ezekiel's Warnings

I can relate to Ezekiel's call. I remember being on a missions trip in Nicaragua and sitting on the top bunk of a hot tin-roofed dorm with unusual critters making unusual noises when the

Lord revealed that part of my purpose was to warn. It was with reverential fear and awe that I read Ezekiel's calling. As I mentioned just a moment ago, I had been delivering prophetic warnings for some time, but I always wished I had something more pleasant to say.

Do not get me wrong; it was not as if the Lord did not speak words of edification and comfort through me. But there was a season early in my ministry during which it seemed I was doing little more than delivering warning after warning after warning. I grew weary of it. I think others did too. It got to the point that when my pastor saw me coming with a prophetic word he seemed to hold his breath. He always received it, but he knew it meant warfare. So when the Lord directed me to Ezekiel's calling, I was both relieved and awestricken by the responsibility. With this revelation, I was able to embrace the call with humility instead of resisting it with dread.

When God called Ezekiel, he was minding his own business, just like Moses was when he encountered the burning bush. Ezekiel was exiled in Babylon with his Hebrew brethren when the Lord opened his eyes to visions of God. He saw the memorable "wheel within a wheel" vision and fell facedown. That is when he heard the voice of one speaking. The Lord told him in Ezekiel 2:3–6:

> And He said to me: Son of man, I send you to the sons of Israel, to a rebellious nation that has rebelled against Me. They and their fathers have transgressed against Me even to this very day. And as for the impudent and obstinate children, I am sending you to them. And you shall say to them, "Thus says the Lord GOD." As for them, whether they listen or not (for they are a rebellious house), they shall know that there has been a prophet among them. And you, son of man, do not be afraid of them or be afraid of their words, though briers and thorns be with you, and you dwell among scorpions. Do not be afraid of their words or be dismayed at their looks, for they are a rebellious house.

Ezekiel's calling brought with it grave responsibility. In the third chapter of Ezekiel we read that God appointed him a watchman to the house of Israel. God told Ezekiel to warn the people about what He was saying to the nation, and He explained the consequences of falling down on the job. Listen in to God's instructions to Ezekiel right before He sent him out with his first prophetic assignment.

Son of man, I have made you a watchman to the house of Israel. Whenever you hear the word from My mouth, then warn them from Me. When I say to the wicked, "You shall surely die," and you do not warn him, nor speak to warn the wicked from his wicked way that he may live, the same wicked man shall die in his iniquity, but his blood I will require at your hand. Yet if you warn the wicked and he does not turn from his wickedness or from his wicked way, he shall die in his iniquity. But you have delivered your soul.

Again, when a righteous man turns from his righteousness and commits iniquity, and I lay a stumbling block before him, he shall die. Because you have not given him warning, he shall die in his sin, and his righteousness which he has done shall not be remembered. But his blood I will require at your hand.

Ezekiel 3:17–20

So we see that Ezekiel's mission was clear from his very calling. If we looked at Jeremiah's call, we would discover his unique mission there as well. The same holds true with Isaiah and other prophets whose callings are recorded in the Bible. Read about prophets like Elisha for yourself and see the test he passed as part of his calling (see 1 Kings 19:21). He left everything and did not look back. Some prophets were called from birth, like Jeremiah and John the Baptist. Others, like Amos, just had a powerful experience with God in the midst of their everyday lives (see Amos 7:10–15).

The important thing to remember is that Jesus gives prophets; the Holy Spirit gives prophecy. No matter how we are called, there is almost always a time of training and making between the calling and the commissioning. Then once we are commissioned and fully active in the prophetic, there is always another level of anointing, accuracy and authority to attain. We must always maintain a sharp prophetic edge. The making process never truly ends. You just keep going from level to level to level—or, as the Bibles says, "from glory to glory" (2 Corinthians 3:18).

Next-Level Prophetic Exercises

Notice that Moses, Samuel and Ezekiel were all prophets of Jehovah. But each was called under drastically different circumstances and with drastically different missions. Moses and Abraham were much older when God called them, for example, than Samuel and Jeremiah were. Meanwhile, Ezekiel was about thirty years old when God called him as a prophet.

Prophetic ministry, then, has foundations and boundaries, but no two prophets are exactly alike. We may have similar callings, but God has a unique plan and a unique mission for each of us. It is up to us to press into it. You can begin with these crucial steps:

✓ Ask the Holy Spirit to unveil your unique mission to the Body of Christ so that you can continue moving from level to level to level, according to His will. Maybe you have already received prophetic words about what God has planned for your ministry. Perhaps you have received a prophetic glimmer of your ultimate purpose. God does not usually tell us all at once. (We probably could not handle it. We would get scared or puffed up in pride.) But I believe He does reveal what we need to know about our callings and missions to motivate us to pay the price to get there.

✓ There are many aspects of prophetic ministry. God calls some with a bent toward reformation, others with a gift for deliverance, still others as seers or prophetic intercessors. Although prophets can function in all of these operations, recognizing how God tends to use you most will help you press into that gifting and further develop it.

✓ Increase the amount of time you spend in prayer and in the Word. No matter what level you are at, this will prepare you to go to the next level.

✓ Consecrate yourself to the Lord and commit to dying to self. Work with the Holy Spirit to prepare your heart.

✓ Feed the gift. Tap into prophetic training resources and other materials that help prepare you for the next level.

✓ Do not get ahead of God, because that will only delay your destiny.

God is depending on His prophets in this hour to answer the call, prepare themselves and complete their missions, while also equipping the next generation to do the same. In the next chapter, we will talk a little bit about what goes into the making of a prophet.

2

The Making of a Prophet

> Before I formed you in the womb I knew [and ap-
> proved of you as My chosen instrument], and be-
> fore you were born I consecrated you [to Myself
> as My own]; I have appointed you as a prophet to
> the nations.
>
> Jeremiah 1:5 AMP

Prophets may be called from their mother's womb, but they
are not born overnight. Prophets go through a making process
that shapes their character and burns off their impurities as
they gain experience in the ways of God.[1]

Before we can get to the next level in prophetic ministry, we
need to experience layers of making. The making never ends,
but I believe we are "made" to a certain level that qualifies us to
stand in the office of the prophet and function in the ministry
with maturity. From there, we can go to higher and higher levels
in prophetic ministry.

Many times the process goes something like this: calling,
making, commissioning. As I mentioned in the first chapter, the

Lord may begin to use us before we are commissioned to our higher calling, even if we are in the early stages of the making process. He uses us where we are during the making process, but not at the level He has planned for us after we have been tried, tested and proven. The process can be frustrating, but it can also be liberating if you learn to yield to God's hand rather than letting impatience cloud your perception of your readiness.

I remember a time when I was frustrated. It seemed to me that others got away with things God would never have allowed me to do; the heart conviction I would have felt would have been far too strong for me to stray into that territory. It seemed there was a double standard—others got double for their trouble, and I just got more trouble. I remember things just did not seem fair, just or right. I asked the Lord about this, and He gave me a revelation of what I was experiencing. It is found in Deuteronomy 8:2–3. I like *The Message* translation, because God talks to me in this manner rather than in *thees* and *thous*:

> Remember every road that GOD led you on for those forty years in the wilderness, pushing you to your limits, testing you so that he would know what you were made of, whether you would keep his commandments or not. He put you through hard times. He made you go hungry. Then he fed you with manna, something neither you nor your parents knew anything about, so you would learn that men and women don't live by bread only; we live by every word that comes from God's mouth.

During this time an elder prophet told me something in line with this Scripture that really helped me. I am going to share it with you. She said, "As a prophet, you have to get everything straight from God. You have to get your appreciation from God. You have to get your recognition from God. You have to get your worth from God. It's you and God." I had to learn how to let God bring vindication for what did not seem right. I had to learn that my path was narrower than some others' and accept—and even appreciate—that. Experiences like these are part of the making. God is just waiting to see how we are going to respond. Ultimately, it is all about learning to trust Him and learning to know His voice and His ways.

Let the Making Begin

For those prophets who are called from their mother's womb, I believe that making starts from the early days of life, whether we ever know it or not. Think back to your childhood. Were you different from other kids? Did you feel like an outcast? Did you deal with rejection? Did you experience trials and temptations that other kids seemed to escape? Could it be possible that the devil was out to derail you and that God was using some of those circumstances to shape you? I believe so.

The devil worked to destroy me since I was four years old through abuse. That abuse left my soul warped, though I would not realize just how warped until much later in life. When I was seven years old, I broke my leg in a freak accident and endured painful traction in a hospital bed for weeks before being wrapped in a body cast. I missed the better part of a year of school and had to learn how to walk all over again. When I was eight years old, I underwent a repeat performance. Same hospital. Same painful traction. Same plaster body cast. Same physical therapy. Needless to say, I was isolated from other children during this time, only able to watch them play outside from my bedroom window. The days were long and lonely.

By my teenage years I was heavy into drugs and alcohol and the lifestyle that went along with them. When I finally settled down, got married and had a baby, my husband soon left the country and his young family. Within a year I lost my husband, my job, my home, my dog, my money and my friends. It sounds like a country song on steroids. But thank God, I found Him, and I soon found my purpose.

I will not recount my entire life's story here. You can read a lot about my testimony in my book *Breakthrough* (Revelation Media Networks, 2011), where I share my miraculous testimony of vindication from false imprisonment and more. I just want to make a point that the devil came early to steal, kill and destroy me, but God's plan and hand of redemption were—and are—greater.

True prophets have a mercy gift and demonstrate great grace, and it is difficult to express mercy and grace if you have never experienced the need for either or received it for yourself. You cannot rightly give away something you have not received.

I say all this to say that the making can start before the calling. You have heard it said this way: "Let your mess become your message." The enemy often senses our calling before we do and tries to take us out of the light and into darkness, including the darkness of divination, the darkness of pain and bitterness and the darkness of rejection. God does not bring all this calamity in our lives, but He can use your life's experience—for better or worse—to shape you and mold you into the prophet He wants you to be.

Cooperating with the Grace of God

While the making of a prophet may indeed begin before the actual calling, it is upon recognition and acceptance of that calling that the Holy Spirit can work with the prophet to begin taking him where He needs him to go. This begins the sharpening.

Whatever happened in your past—whether you were born into the church or stumbled upon Jesus despite yourself, like I did—there comes a time in every prophet's life when the prophetic calling becomes clear. It could be that God revealed this to you personally or that He sent another prophet to make the announcement. At this stage, a new level of sharpening begins. Whereas you may have resisted God out of pure ignorance as a lost soul or a baby Christian, when God makes this prophetic calling clear to you, He expects a greater level of cooperation with this making process.

Young prophets must learn to hear the voice of the Lord. That is why God told Jeremiah to "go down to the potter's house" (Jeremiah 18:1–4). But notice Jeremiah's cooperation. He had to obey the Lord's command to arise and go down to the potter's house. Too often prophets fail to make time to visit the potter's house. That shows in their character and in their public ministry with dry or inaccurate utterances. Even mature prophets have to go back to the potter's house. The experience helps us to hear God's words more clearly as we are chiseled more into His image.

Some people receive a calling to the office of the prophet and run out to the copy center the next day to get some business cards and start a ministry. They assume the title without understanding the function, and many times they bring a reproach on true prophetic giftings with their immature behavior. Mature prophets, however, follow prophetic protocols. You will cooperate with God through an extensive training process that includes practical lessons and experience in spiritual warfare, deliverance, prayer and intercession and the role of the prophet in a local assembly.

The Extensive Training Process

If young prophets would seek out balanced training resources from legitimate prophetic ministers with proven ministries, we would see a much more stable prophetic movement today. The making process is not intended to make you into a prophetic rock star. The making process is not to make you into a millionaire. The making process is to teach you and train you in prophetic protocols while also breaking off impurities like pride, independence, and rebellion. It is a time for working in you holiness, integrity, generosity, obedience, commitment, mercy and love for the unlovely.

The point is, we have to learn to walk before we learn to run. God will take us through a making—or sometimes even a remaking—to undo the damage religious thinking has done. Ultimately, the same lessons you learn during the making process are the same pursuits that will help you sharpen your prophetic edge.

After this initial making and training, it becomes a matter of continuing to press in. The Lord once told me this: "You have to go deeper to go higher." If you want to get to a higher level in the prophetic, that means going deeper into God. That does not mean working up deep, dark sayings to impress folks in church. It means deepening your relationship with Him.

On another occasion the Lord told me, "If you want to know more, spend more time with Me." We get our counsel from the Lord. We get our prophetic utterances from the Lord. We get everything from the Lord. If we want to go higher, we have to go deeper in Him to find the mysteries that are hidden in Christ. If we want to hear and see more, we need to consecrate ourselves to Him at another level.

Do Not Be a Spoiled Vessel

Since there are many, many levels of prophetic maturity, this next-level process lasts a lifetime. No matter how accurate you are, how many miracles are wrought in your ministry or how many people know your name, prophets never arrive. We never get off the potter's wheel, because we will not be finished until Jesus comes back to get us. If we get off into excessive pride, disobedience or rebellion, God will simply crush the clay and start over.

When Jeremiah went down to the potter's house, he saw him working at the wheel. But the pot he was shaping from the clay was marred in his hands, so the potter formed it into another pot, shaping it as seemed best to him. Let's read these verses from Jeremiah 18:1–4:

> The word which came to Jeremiah from the LORD, saying: "Arise and go down to the potter's house, and there I will cause you to hear My words." Then I went down to the potter's house, and there he was making something on the wheel. Yet the vessel that he made of clay was spoiled in the hand of the potter; so he made it again into another vessel, as seemed good to the potter to make it.

Now, if the vessel is marred, it is not the potter's fault. We know God does not make mistakes. Think about it for a minute. Could it be possible that the clay resisted the making process and so was marred? And if so, could it be possible that the clay missed its first and highest calling when the potter started over? The Bible says God made it into another vessel. Those kinds of thoughts bring a reverential fear of God into my heart.

We must not resist the hand of the Potter. No matter what level we find ourselves at—and no matter how painful it is—we must be careful to keep pressing in to God. Dying flesh is always painful, but the result is always worth it. When we crucify our flesh, God gives us newness of life. When we walk in the flesh, our prophetic edge grows dull.

You have heard it said, "No pain; no gain." That is true in the things of God too. Progress in God always costs you something. Sometimes it is more painful than others. But here's the mystery: It may look far too expensive, but you are really getting a basement bargain. In other words, the price only seems too much to pay because of your limited perspective. God knows what we can pay, and He does not require a higher cost than we can afford.

Next-Level Prophetic Exercises

The making process is all about cooperating with the Holy Spirit. Your best step forward is to spend time with Him, examine your heart for root issues that could hinder, muddy or even pervert your prophetic gifting, and let Him show you what He wants to work on—or work out—in your soul or flesh. This is an ongoing process.

✓ Ask Him to make your heart and ears sensitive to His leading and His voice so that you can lay down sins and weights that so easily best you (see Hebrews 12:1).

✓ Count the costs of going to the next level of prophetic ministry—and be willing to pay the price.

✓ Determine in your heart to submit to the making process, no matter how painful it may be to your soul and your flesh. Do not resist the hand of the Potter.

✓ Learn to discern between demonic pressure that you need to resist and godly pressure to which you need to submit.

In the next chapter, we will explore the unconditional prerequisite for prophets who want to move to the next level with a sharp prophetic edge: obedience.

3

Obedience: The Prophet's Prerequisite

> Does the LORD delight in burnt offerings and sacri-
> fices as much as in obeying the voice of the LORD?
> Obedience is better than sacrifice, a listening ear
> than the fat of rams.
>
> 1 Samuel 15:22

Are you obedient to do all the Lord commands you to do? Let me put it another way. Are you quickly obedient to all the Lord's commands? When He tells you to do something, do you hem and haw and try to find a way to squirm out of it? Do you reason out why it could not possibly be God instructing you to do what He is instructing you to do? Do you argue with God about it, make excuses or procrastinate? Or do you work with the Holy Spirit to develop an action plan to execute the strategy God has spoken in His timing?

Obedience is better than sacrifice. Indeed, obedience is the prophet's prerequisite. Your obedience builds the Lord's trust in you. God will often give His prophets small—or even strange—instructions. Step by step, obeying God's voice will transition you from low-level assignments to next-level missions. Disobeying God's voice could land you in the belly of a whale. (You remember Jonah, right?)

People like to point to the stereotypical mule when they speak of stubbornness. But have you considered Balaam's talking donkey? He had more sense than the old prophet, and God spoke through him (see Numbers 22:28). Balaam was headed out of God's will. When the donkey saw the angel of the Lord standing in the road, he turned and went into a field. The donkey was submissive enough to obey what he perceived as the Lord's will. What did Balaam do? He whacked the donkey good (see Numbers 22:25).

The moral of the story: Prophets can be more stubborn than the stereotypical donkey. Do not let that be you!

Abram's Delayed Obedience

Abraham is known as the father of faith. He is also recognized as a prophet in Scripture (see Genesis 20:7). But Abram struggled from time to time with God's instructions. Yes, he was a man of God and a prophet, and he was obedient to the word of the Lord to leave his hometown and go to a land God would show him (see Genesis 12:1). But he was not one-hundred-percent obedient from the get-go, and it caused him a few problems. Let's take a look at how Abram sharpened his prophetic edge after a few hindrances that sprang up when he did not execute every jot and tittle of God's initial instruction.

> Now the Lord said to Abram, "Go from your country, your family, and your father's house to the land that I will show you. I will make of you a great nation; I will bless you and make your name great, so that you will be a blessing. I will bless them who

bless you and curse him who curses you, and in you all families of the earth will be blessed." So Abram departed, as the LORD had spoken to him, and Lot went with him.

Genesis 12:1–4

Read that again. What did God say? God specifically told Abram to go out from his family. That means do not bring your nieces and nephews and cousins and uncles—but Abram allowed Lot to come along for the ride. Abram compromised at the beginning of his journey into God's promise and would eventually pay a price.

What is interesting is that Moses, who penned these verses by the inspiration of the Holy Spirit, emphasized again how Lot was with Abram in Genesis 13:1, almost like a reminder of Abram's less-than-total obedience. The verse reads, "So Abram went up from Egypt to the Negev, he and his wife and all that he had, and Lot with him." We see yet another mention of Lot in Genesis 13:5, where the Holy Spirit specifically points a third time to "Lot, who went with Abram."

If I have learned anything, it is that partial obedience leads to problems. Partial obedience is better than no obedience, but partial obedience leaves room for the enemy's devices and can dull your prophetic edge.

The issue is that Lot was a *went* one, not a sent one. (That is an entirely different topic for prophetic people, but the short lesson is to make sure when you feel led it is really God doing the leading.) Please understand, it was not as if Abram necessarily invited Lot to come with him on this journey. Rather, I get the impression Lot went with him, and Abram did not stop him from tagging along. Nevertheless, Abram was less than one-hundred-percent obedient, and ultimately there is no excuse to justify disobedience.

Now Lot, who went with Abram, also had flocks and herds and tents. But the land was not able to support them both dwelling together because their possessions were so great. And there was strife between the herdsmen of Abram's livestock and the herdsmen of Lot's livestock.

Genesis 13:5–7

God made plenty of provision for Abram and his flocks and herds and tents in that land—but He did not plan for Lot to go with him and raise his own livestock to graze those same fields. When we move out in less than full obedience to God, He is not obligated to provide for the excess. Read that again. When we move out in less than full obedience to God, He is not obligated to provide for the excess.

What happened? It did not take long for a spirit of strife to attack Abram and Lot.

When God Is Silent

I do not know if Abram got a revelation, if he remembered God's instruction to go from his family or if he was just trying to be a peacemaker, but Abram definitely made his next move in the wisdom of God.

So Abram said to Lot, "Let there be no strife, I ask you, between me and you, and between my herdsmen and your herdsmen, for we are close relatives. Is not the whole land before you? Please separate from me. If you will go to the left, then I will go to the right, or if you take the right, then I will go to the left."

Genesis 13:8–9

Now, catch this. The Bible says Abram built an altar to the Lord and called on the name of the Lord after Lot came with him on his journey (see Genesis 12:7). No answer. In fact, he immediately ran into warfare when Pharaoh took his wife and he told Sarai to lie and say she was his sister to spare his life. One compromise—allowing Lot to come with him—led to another compromise, lying. See how that works?

Abram again built an altar and called on the name of the Lord some time later, as recorded in Genesis 13:4. There is no "The word of the Lord came unto Abram saying . . ." that follows. It was not until after Lot departed that God spoke to Abram again. God's grace covered Abram's less than full obedience and confirmed the covenant was still in place (see Genesis 13:14), but Abram went an entire chapter of his life without hearing the voice of the Lord.

I do not know about you, but I do not want to go a whole chapter in my life without hearing from God. I live by every word that proceeds out of His mouth (see Matthew 4:4). I want my prophetic edge to be as sharp as possible. Prophets cannot function in their calling—much less get to the next level—without hearing the voice of the Lord.

If we want to sharpen our prophetic edge and cut through to the next level, we have to be obedient to do all of what God says, not just part of it. Abram was obedient to go away from his country, but he was not fully obedient to leave his family behind. As a result, God sat by and watched—in silence. Yes, God was surely with him, as He will never leave us or forsake us (see Hebrews 13:5). But disobedience to a direct instruction from Jehovah can cause Him to sit back and wait for you to right the wrong before He will give you another word.

Put another way, sometimes God is silent until we choose to act in faith and in obedience to the last word He spoke. So if you are in a silent season, think back to what He said to you last and set your heart to walk in the fullness of that word.

Jeremiah's Full Obedience

In contrast, Jeremiah was obedient each step of the way. Although he initially questioned God's call, protesting that he was just a youth, once he accepted the calling and the commissioning, he progressed from one level to another through obedience and the grace of God, even in the face of persecution. There is a strong example of Jeremiah's attention to every minute detail of God's instruction in Jeremiah 13:1–17:

> Thus says the LORD to me, "Go and buy yourself a linen waistband and put it upon your loins, and do not put it in water." So I bought a waistband according to the word of the LORD and put it on my loins.
>
> The word of the LORD came to me the second time, saying, "Take the waistband that you have, which is upon your loins, and arise, go to the Euphrates and hide it there in a hole of the rock." So I went and hid it by the Euphrates, as the LORD had commanded me.
>
> After many days the LORD said to me, "Arise, go to the Euphrates and take the waistband from there, which I commanded you to hide there." Then I went to the Euphrates, and dug, and took the waistband from the place where I had hidden it. But the waistband was destroyed. It was profitable for nothing.
>
> Then the word of the LORD came to me: Thus says the LORD: After this manner I will destroy the pride of Judah and the great pride of Jerusalem. This evil people, who refuse to hear My words, who walk in the imagination of their hearts, and walk after other gods, to serve them, and to worship them, shall be even as this waistband which is good for nothing. For as the waistband cleaves to the loins of a man, so I have caused the whole house of Israel and the whole house of Judah to cleave to Me, says the LORD, so that they might be to Me a people for renown, and for a praise, and for a glory; but they would not listen.
>
> Therefore you shall speak to them this word: Thus says the LORD God of Israel: Every bottle shall be filled with wine. And when they say to you, "Do we not certainly know that every bottle should be filled with wine?" then you shall say to them: Thus says the LORD: I will fill all the inhabitants of this land—even the kings that sit on the throne of David, and the priests, and the prophets, and all the inhabitants of Jerusalem—with

drunkenness. I will dash them against one another, even the fathers and the sons together, says the LORD. I will not show pity nor spare nor have mercy, but will destroy them. Hear and give heed; do not be proud, for the LORD has spoken. Give glory to the LORD your God, before He causes darkness and before your feet stumble on the dark mountains, and while you look for light, He turns it into the shadow of death and makes it gross darkness. But if you will not listen to it, my soul will weep in secret places for your pride; and my eyes will weep sorely and run down with tears, because the flock of the LORD is carried away captive.

Again, notice how Jeremiah was obedient to each little instruction. He did not speak before the Lord told him to speak. He was not happy or prideful to deliver the warning. This is an example of the hundredfold obedience God wants from His prophets and prophetic voices. The more obedient you are to His instructions, the faster you will go to the next level. Although this is not a race to the top, you certainly do not want to wander around the mountain in disobedience.

A Prophetic Call to the Valley of Shechem

If you are reading these words, then you have probably already chosen this day whom you will serve. But could it be possible that there are yet things you need to put away in order to truly worship the Lord in spirit and in truth and love Him with all your heart, with all your soul, with all your strength and with all your mind? I submit to you that it is possible—and for many of us even probable—that something is getting in the way of greater obedience that will take you to the next level of your prophetic calling.

Today the Lord is calling you to the Valley of Shechem. Previously, I had not spent much time studying the rich biblical history of the Valley of Shechem, the place where Abraham first built an altar to the Lord on his migration out of an idolatrous land. I had never done an intense analysis of this valley between Mounts Ebal and Gerizim, where Jacob built his well and Jesus would later tell a woman everything she ever did (see John 4).

No, I did not know too much about this significant valley. But it only took three words from the Lord to pique my curiosity. He said to me, "Valley of Shechem." Those three words set me off on a prophetic investigation for what the Lord is saying to the Church. I studied the geographical and historical significance of Shechem, but it was the spiritual significance on which the Lord shined a bright light.

The Valley of Shechem is where Joshua called together all the tribes of Israel. Once all the elders, chiefs, judges and officers arrived and presented themselves before God, Joshua delivered a powerful prophetic word to the nation (see Joshua 24). Joshua prophesied about Abraham, a prophet who once worshiped other gods. He prophesied about the plagues on Egypt. He prophesied about the parting of the Red Sea. He essentially offered a history of Israel right up to its modern day. God was reminding them of the kind intentions of His will.

God was going somewhere with this prophetic history lesson. Indeed, He was methodically working to drive home a point. See, God had given Israel a land for which she did not labor and cities she did not build. Israel was dwelling safely in the Promised Land, eating of the vineyards and the olive groves. In other words, God followed His miraculous deliverance with His abundant grace. Much the same, God "has blessed us with every spiritual blessing in heavenly places in Christ . . . predestined us to adoption as sons to Himself through Jesus Christ according to the good pleasure of His will" (Ephesians 1:3, 5).

Applying the Prophetic Message

With this spiritual truth in mind, come with me to the Valley of Shechem and listen closely to the heart of the prophetic message Joshua delivered to Israel on that day of decision, and then apply it to yourself.

> "Now therefore, fear the LORD, serve Him in sincerity and in truth, and put away the gods which your fathers served on the other side of the River and in Egypt. Serve the LORD! And if it seems evil to you to serve the LORD, choose for yourselves this day whom you will serve, whether the gods which your fathers served that were on the other side of the River, or the gods of the Amorites, in whose land you dwell. But as for me and my house, we will serve the LORD."
>
> Joshua 24:14–15 NKJV

The question is simple: Will you serve Jehovah with whole-hearted obedience, or will you serve some idol? The simplest definition of *idol* is "a false god." *Merriam-Webster* defines *idol* as a "representation or symbol of an object of worship; a false god." Another definition is "pretender, impostor." Yet another definition is "an object of extreme devotion" or "a false conception."

In ancient times, people created idols to worship. They gave these wooden, silver and golden idols names that represented gods. Today, we are a little more sophisticated, and the enemy is a little subtler. We would never dream of worshiping a golden calf. That is blatant disobedience. But we may be tempted to worship our favorite sport, our career, our children or even our ministry. We may be tempted to put off what the Lord is calling us to do to serve one of these idols.

In other words, we may set up people, places and things as idols in our lives that draw our attention away from God's will. Anything that draws our attention away from Jesus is a pretender and an imposter. Any object of extreme devotion apart from God is a false god.

The Bible clearly says, "You shall have no other gods before Me" (Exodus 20:3). In case you did not hear it loud and clear

51

in Exodus, the Holy Spirit repeats Himself in Deuteronomy 5:7: "You shall have no other gods before Me." He says it once more in Exodus 34:14 (KJV): "For thou shalt worship no other god: for the LORD, whose name is Jealous, is a jealous God." When we disobey God, we are putting some other god before Him. Sometimes it is self, which we will talk about in an upcoming chapter.

Disobedience Can Be Dangerous

God commands obedience to His Word because He has our best interests at heart. God's "commandments are not burdensome" (1 John 5:3)—they protect us from Satan's deadly traps. James 1:22 warns us, "Be doers of the word and not hearers only, deceiving yourselves." The prophet Daniel determined in his heart to be obedient to God even when it landed him in a lion's den (see Daniel 6). His obedience turned God's head, and Jehovah delivered him.

Of course, it is absolutely vital that every believer obey the Word of God, but it can be a dangerous proposition for prophets to disobey the voice of the Lord. Jonah is a good example. God commanded him to go to Nineveh with a message of repentance. He did not like the assignment, so he ran in the opposite direction God was sending him (see Jonah 1:1–3). You know the story. The stubborn prophet ended up in the belly of a whale. If he had not repented, that would have been the end of the story. Thankfully, Jonah came to his senses and changed his mind (see Jonah 3:3).

But there is another prophet in Scripture who did not have that opportunity, a man of God whom Jehovah used to teach a king a lesson. God told the prophet to go to Bethel and cry out against the altar by the word of the Lord. He prophesied to King Jeroboam that the altar would be torn apart and the ashes atop it would be poured out. The prophet obeyed God despite the danger that comes with offending a king. Let's listen in to what happened next from 1 Kings 13:4–10:

> When King Jeroboam heard the saying of the man of God who had cried against the altar in Bethel, he reached out his hand from the altar, saying, "Arrest him!" And the hand that he put forth against him dried up so that he could not pull it back in again. The altar also was torn, and the ashes poured out from the altar, just as the man of God had said it would as a sign of the LORD.
>
> The king answered and said to the man of God, "Seek the face of the LORD your God, and pray for me, that my hand will be healed." And the man of God interceded with the LORD, and the king's hand was healed and became as it was before. The king said to the man of God, "Come home with me and refresh yourself, and I will give you a reward."
>
> The man of God said to the king, "If you were to give me half your house, I would not go with you, nor will I eat bread nor drink water in this place, for so I was commanded by the word of the LORD, saying: You shall eat no bread, nor drink water nor return by the same way that you came." So he went another way and did not return by the same way he came to Bethel.

Tucked away in that passage is another command. The Lord told the prophet to "eat no bread, nor drink water nor return by the same way that you came" (verse 9). The prophet started out in obedience to that word by refusing the king's offer, but then something odd happened. An old prophet in Bethel heard about the man of God's encounter with the king, climbed on his donkey and went after him.

"Are you the man of God who came from Judah?"

And he said, "I am."

Then he said to him, "Come home with me and eat bread."

He said, "I may not return with you or go in with you, nor will I eat bread nor drink water with you in this place, for I was

53

commanded by the word of the LORD: You shall eat no bread and drink no water there nor return by the way you came."

1 Kings 13:14–17

Here we see the younger prophet holding fast to obedience. He was probably tired and hungry, but he chose obedience to God over the desires of his flesh. But this old prophet deceived him.

He said to him, "I am a prophet like you, and an angel spoke to me by the word of the LORD, saying, 'Bring him back with you into your house so that he may eat bread and drink water.'" But he had lied to him. So he went back with him to his house and ate bread and drank water.

1 Kings 13:18–19

Let me take you on a quick bunny trail here. I believe angels can come and bring messages from God to prophets or anyone else He sends them to visit. But if that angel carries a message that violates the written Word of God, then that angel did not come from God. Paul the apostle warned us that "Satan disguises himself as an angel of light" (2 Corinthians 11:14). Paul also admonished:

Do not let anyone cheat you of your reward by delighting in false humility and the worship of angels, dwelling on those things which he has not seen, vainly arrogant due to his unspiritual mind, and not supporting the head, from which the entire body, nourished and knit together by joints and sinews, grows as God gives the increase.

Colossians 2:18–19

And let's not forget Paul's words in Galatians 1:8 about the curse on anyone—even an angel in heaven—who preaches a false gospel. Again, I believe in angels, and I believe angels can visit people with messages, but there is an overemphasis on angels in the prophetic movement that troubles me. I am concerned these "angelic visitations" are leading some astray, and the end could be disobedience.

Of course, the young prophet did not have the benefit of Paul's revelations. Let's take a look at the rest of this unfortunate story:

> Then as they sat at the table, the word of the LORD came to the prophet who brought him back, and he cried out to the man of God who came from Judah, saying, "Thus says the LORD: Since you have disobeyed the mouth of the LORD and have not kept the commandment that the LORD your God commanded you, but instead came back and have eaten bread and drunk water in the place of which the LORD told you to eat no bread and drink no water, your carcass will not be buried in the tomb of your fathers!"
>
> After he had eaten bread and had drunk, he saddled the donkey for the prophet whom he had brought back. As he was going, a lion met him on the way and killed him, and his body was thrown in the road, and both the donkey and lion stood by it. Some men passed by and saw the body thrown in the road with the lion standing by the body, and they came and told the story in the city where the old prophet lived.
>
> When the prophet who brought him back from the way heard about it, he said, "It is the man of God who was disobedient to the word of the LORD, and thus the LORD has delivered him to the lion, which has torn and slain him, according to the word of the LORD that He spoke to him."
>
> 1 Kings 13:20–26

So let's review. This young prophet was especially accurate. This young prophet stood before a king and delivered a powerful prophecy with a sign and a miracle. This young prophet held fast to his obedience until he met another prophet who led him astray based on the revelation of an angel. The young prophet's disobedience not only cost him his life, but he goes down in Bible history as "the man of God who was disobedient to the word of the LORD" (1 Kings 13:26). What an unfortunate legacy! It does not always take a deceptive prophet or an angel to lead believers into disobedience. In fact, it is usually much easier than that. Let's remember this: Jesus said if we love Him, we will keep His commandments (see John 14:15) and questioned why some called Him "Lord" but would not do what He told them (see Luke 6:46).

If you want to get to the next level, obey God in every little thing He tells you to do, and if you fail to obey completely, be quick to repent. It is doubtful that you will meet a false prophet who lies about an angelic vision to deceive you, but there is really no need for all that fanfare because, like James 1:22 says, if we hear the Word and do not do it, we deceive ourselves.

Next-Level Prophetic Exercises

Even though He was the Son of God, the Bible tells us Jesus "learned obedience through the things that He suffered" (Hebrews 5:8). Suffering does teach us lessons, like what not to do again and what to do instead. Although we cannot avoid all suffering in life, I believe we can suffer less by learning from examples God left in Scripture. Since obedience is a key to your next level, spend some time with these exercises.

✓ Take some time to study and learn from Abram's delayed obedience, Jeremiah's full obedience and the consequences for disobediences displayed on the pages of Holy Scripture. This will serve as a motivator for you to pursue hundredfold obedience.

✓ Ask the Holy Spirit to reveal any areas of disobedience in your life. You may not know you are directly disobeying the will of the Lord in some area because of

deception. James 1:22 tells us plainly that if we hear the
Word but do not do the Word, we have deceived ourselves. Take this to heart.

✓ With James 1:22 in mind, ask the Lord to break off any
deception from your mind.

✓ Ask the Lord for the grace of obedience. Titus 2:11–14
tells us:

> For the grace of God that brings salvation has appeared to all
> men, teaching us that, denying ungodliness and worldly desires,
> we should live soberly, righteously, and in godliness in this pres-
> ent world, as we await the blessed hope and the appearing of
> the glory of our great God and Savior Jesus Christ, who gave
> Himself for us, that He might redeem us from all lawlessness
> and purify for Himself a special people, zealous of good works.

✓ Ask the Lord if there are any sins of omission in your
life. Sins of commission are sins that you actively commit, such as lying, gossiping and the like. Sins of omission are sins relating to scriptural commands that you
do not carry out. James 4:17 exhorts, "Therefore, to
him who knows to do good and does not do it, it is
sin."

✓ When you miss it in the area of obedience, do not allow
the enemy to condemn, guilt and shame you. Run to the
throne of grace and receive forgiveness and strength to
keep fighting.

Obedience is one thing. Willingness is another. Willingness is
insurance against disobedience. Prophets must be willing to
carry spiritual burdens to get to higher levels of the prophetic.
In the next chapter, we will explore a willing heart, which is an
important companion to obedience.

4

Willingness: The Prophet's Insurance Policy

> If you are willing and obedient, you shall eat the good of the land; but if you refuse and rebel, you shall be devoured with the sword; for the mouth of the LORD has spoken it.
>
> Isaiah 1:19–20

"Willingness is insurance against disobedience." The Holy Spirit once spoke those words to my heart at a time when I was being pressed to follow Him at a deeper level. I had to meditate on those words for a little while to get the full meaning. Here is the revelation I received: If you are willing, you will obey. If you are not willing, you may obey for a while because you know it is the right thing to do, but your flesh or soul will eventually rebel because your will is not with you. Put differently, "The spirit . . . is willing, but the flesh is weak" (Mark 14:38).

God gave us a free will, but He wants us to submit our will to His will even when our flesh or emotions or reasoning do not agree with Him. Sometimes God asks us to do things that seem contrary to His plan for our lives. We need to trust Him and be fully willing to obey. Sometimes God asks us to do things that seem scary to our souls. We need to walk in faith and be fully willing to obey. Sometimes God asks us to do things that come at a cost to our personal lives. We need to count the costs and be willing to obey. Willingness is insurance against disobedience.

We cannot serve God and our flesh at the same time. "No one can serve two masters" (Luke 16:13 NLT). The mind governed by the flesh is hostile to God. It has never obeyed God's commands, nor is it willing to (see Romans 8:7). We have to make a decision by our will to die to ourselves, to crucify our flesh with its affections and lusts, to pick up our cross and follow Him. We have to be willing to do these things. It is insurance against disobedience. Willingness does not mean we will not stumble and fall, but it does ensure that if we do stumble and fall, we will be quick to repent, realign our will and renew our insurance policy.

The Parable of the Two Sons

Let me say this again: Willingness is insurance against disobedience. Jesus offered us a great example of this in the Parable of the Two Sons. Let's listen to Jesus tell it in His own words from Matthew 21:28–31:

> "What do you think? A man had two sons. He came to the first and said, 'Son, go work today in my vineyard.' He answered, 'I will not,' but afterward he repented and went. Then he came to the second, and said likewise. He answered, 'I will go, sir,' but did not go. Which of the two did the will of his father?" They said, "The first."

The disciples answered correctly. So many believers are quick to agree with the word of the Lord—the seed of God sown in their hearts—but they do not follow through. Jesus explains why in the Parable of the Sower.

I will not take the time here to recount the whole parable. Suffice it to say that in some cases Satan comes to steal the word that was sown in believers' hearts. Other times they have no root in themselves, so they cannot endure in obedience. Still other times they become unwilling to continue when affliction or persecution arises or when the cares of the world, the deceitfulness of riches or the desire for other things chokes out their willingness (see Mark 4:13–19).

Only those who are willing to cultivate the seed of the Word despite warfare, distractions, trials and carnal desires see that seed bear fruit—some thirty-, sixty- or a hundredfold (see Mark 4:20). Prophets, you need to be willing to cultivate the Word of God in your heart. It will make you willing.

Ezekiel: The Next-Level Prophet

Ezekiel carried many spiritual burdens for Israel. He became part of the prophetic word, acting out the word of the Lord and actually living it. What is interesting about Ezekiel's ministry—beyond all the strange prophetic acts—is how his anointing changed and grew over the course of his ministry. He progressed in his calling to higher and higher levels with more responsibility.

When we meet Ezekiel, he is a priest serving in the fifth year of captivity under King Jehoiachin in the land of the Chaldeans by the River Kebar. The Bible tells us the hand of the Lord was on him there, and he had a vision of God's glory (see Ezekiel 1). This is the well-known "wheel within a wheel" vision that lasted all of Ezekiel 1, concluding with the priest hearing a voice. Ezekiel 2 opens with Jehovah calling Ezekiel the priest into the prophetic ministry.

> And He said to me: Son of man, I send you to the sons of Israel, to a rebellious nation that has rebelled against Me. They and their fathers have transgressed against Me even to this very day.

61

And as for the impudent and obstinate children, I am sending you to them. And you shall say to them, "Thus says the Lord GOD." As for them, whether they listen or not (for they are a rebellious house), they shall know that there has been a prophet among them.

Ezekiel 2:3–5

God knew that in Ezekiel's new role as prophet, fear would come to hinder him from getting to the next level. God warned him not to be afraid of others' words or dismayed by their looks and to speak whether they listened or not.

Ezekiel became a messenger for the Lord who was willing to carry the burden of the Lord through extreme prophetic acts, including eating a scroll. Ezekiel ate a scroll upon which God had written words of lamentation, mourning and woe. God offered the scroll symbolically, and Ezekiel demonstrated his willingness to serve the Lord fully through his willingness to eat the scroll.

Moreover He said to me, Son of man, eat what you find. Eat this scroll and go speak to the house of Israel. So I opened my mouth, and He fed me this scroll. He said to me, Son of man, feed your stomach and fill your inward parts with this scroll that I give you. Then I ate it, and it was as honey for sweetness in my mouth. Then He said to me: Son of man, go to the house of Israel and speak with My words to them.

Ezekiel 3:1–4

Ezekiel got to the next level by his willingness—and his willingness would take him to new levels still. A willing Ezekiel started with a priest's anointing, then received a prophet's anointing and then received a watchman's anointing. This is the "blood is on your hands" commissioning:

At the end of seven days, the word of the LORD came to me, saying, Son of man, I have made you a watchman to the house of Israel. Whenever you hear the word from My mouth, then warn them from Me. When I say to the wicked, "You shall surely die," and you do not warn him, nor speak to warn the wicked from his wicked way that he may live, the same wicked man shall die in his iniquity, but his blood I will require at your hand. Yet if you warn the wicked and he does not turn from his wickedness or from his wicked way, he shall die in his iniquity. But you have delivered your soul.

Again, when a righteous man turns from his righteousness and commits iniquity, and I lay a stumbling block before him, he shall die. Because you have not given him warning, he shall die in his sin, and his righteousness which he has done shall not be remembered. But his blood I will require at your hand. Nevertheless if you warn the righteous man that the righteous should not sin and he does not sin, he shall surely live because he took warning. And you have delivered your soul.

Ezekiel 3:16–21

Ezekiel got to the next level because he was willing and obedient. Most of us never experience the supernatural swirl that Ezekiel witnessed with winged angels and wheels within wheels and the like. But I believe he needed those encounters to fulfill his radical calling. Think about it for a minute. God called him to lie down on his left side for 390 days to bear the guilt of the house of Israel and then on his right side for forty days to bear the guilt of the house of Judah (see Ezekiel 4). He dined on barley cakes baked over cow manure (see Ezekiel 4). He prophesied over a valley of dry bones (see Ezekiel 37). He was willing to look like a fool for the glory of God. That is one way to get to the next level.

Of course, God gets all the glory for our willingness. He works in us, both to will and to work for "His good pleasure" (Philippians 2:13). He has equipped us with everything good so we can "do His will" (Hebrews 13:21). It was not until later in his ministry that God told Ezekiel, "I will put My Spirit within you and cause you to walk in My statutes, and you will keep My judgments and do them" (Ezekiel 36:27). We have the Spirit even now.

Prophets, if you are going to follow Christ into your highest calling, you need to be willing to deny yourself, as Ezekiel did, and then pick up your cross and follow Jesus. He is the prototype Prophet.

Are You Willing to Birth God's Dreams?

God has a dream, and He is looking for prophets and prophetic people who will catch His vision, seek the intimacy with Him that leaves them impregnated with purpose, carry that spiritual baby full term and press through the travail of delivery for His glory. Of course, the Holy Spirit is a gentleman, and He will not force His will on you. If you want to be a vessel God uses to birth His plans and purposes into the earth, you need to be willing. God taught me that lesson through a dream.

Some years ago I had a somewhat perplexing dream. In the dream, I found myself pregnant and was stressed, afraid and confused. After all, I was not married and was living a holy life. I imagine I felt kind of like Mary, the mother of Jesus, who was a virgin betrothed to Joseph when the angel Gabriel came to her with an unexpected prophetic announcement. In the dream, I hoped I was having a bad dream or perhaps I had just packed on a few pounds, but there was no getting around the growing baby bump.

In my dream, I was battling in my mind over the changes a newborn baby would bring into my life. The thoughts of change and sacrifice were overwhelming. I was too old to start over. I had too many responsibilities as it was and would have no help whatsoever with what I saw as an unwelcomed complication. After this mind battle raged for some time, I finally accepted my fate. I finally surrendered to the coming life-altering transition.

When I woke up, the first thing I did was look at my midsection with great relief that it was indeed only a dream. I am a little too spiritually keen to dismiss it as a pizza dream—the phrase I use to describe a dream induced by eating spicy food too late at night. I knew God was speaking to me through this dream as He had so many other baby dreams.

The Holy Spirit Helps Us Surrender

I pondered the dream. I prayed about the dream. I shared the dream with others who have the gift of interpretation. Many times, though, the Lord points me to Scripture to reveal to me what He is saying in my dreams. Remember, I said in the dream I felt like Mary who became pregnant by immaculate conception. So I went to the account of Christ's birth announcement in Luke 1:26–38.

When Mary had this prophetic encounter, the Bible reveals "she was troubled" and Gabriel told her "do not be afraid." Those were my exact emotions in the dream. See, sometimes God's will seems troublesome to our soul and brings fearful emotions. Sometimes, like Mary, we feel that accomplishing the will of God is impossible. Like Mary, we feel that surrendering to His plan could be too costly.

Mary asked, "How can this be . . . ?" (Luke 1:34). Essentially, Gabriel's answer was, "Holy Ghost." As Jesus would later say, "The things which are impossible with men are possible with God" (Luke 18:27 NKJV). All God needs is our yes. When we submit our will to His will, the Holy Spirit will do for us what He did for Mary: come upon us and overshadow us (Luke 1:35).

What seems overwhelming or fearful when we reason it out with our mind becomes pleasing and joyful when we surrender to God's will like Mary did. Mary told Gabriel: "Behold the maidservant of the Lord! Let it be to me according to your word" (Luke 1:38 NKJV).

Engaging in Next-Level Surrender

If you want to become a next-level prophet, you will surrender something to get there. You will have to be willing to drink the cup the Lord gives you, whether that means surrendering some entertainment or surrendering a relationship or surrendering to a season of persecution without retaliating. Old Testament prophets who spoke in the name of the Lord surrendered their comfort, their safety and sometimes their lives to do the will of the Lord. Why should we expect anything different?

Over the years, I have had to realign my will with His will more times than I can count. I have had to follow His will out of corporate America and into full-time ministry, out of my comfortable home and into the mission fields, and more. If you are going to birth your next-level prophetic ministry, you will have some stretch marks, some birth pains and some agony in dying to your flesh along the way, but it is worth it.

If you find yourself unwilling in any area where the Lord is challenging you, ask Him to make you willing to be willing. His grace is sufficient even for this. I believe God is calling prophets like Ezekiel, Jeremiah and Isaiah who are willing to lay it all down for Him. I believe He is calling women like Anna and Deborah and Mary who are willing and obedient to allow the Lord to do what He pleases for His glory. Notice I say for His glory. Mary gave birth to Jesus not for herself but so the sin of the world could be taken away. It was not about Mary. Prophets, it is not about you. Once it becomes about you, it is not about Him, and He has no obligation to bend to your will. We are supposed to bend to His.

Next-Level Prophetic Exercises

As I was coming up in the prophetic, I was not always willing to do everything the Lord asked me to do. He is gracious. He understands we are in process—His process. I had to purify my motives, battle against fear and more. Consider these actions to help you come up higher in your willingness, abandoning your will to His will in every area of your life.

✓ Ask the Lord to reveal the motives of your heart. Are you obeying begrudgingly? Have you said yes to the Lord but failed to complete what He told you to do because in your heart you really did not want to?

✓ Fear can be a root of unwillingness. Ask the Lord to deliver you from fear. Meditate on His perfect love. First John 4:18 assures us that "there is no fear in love, but perfect love casts out fear, because fear has to do with punishment. Whoever fears is not perfect in love."

✓ Procrastination can be a sign of fear or dread, but it can also be a sign of unwillingness. Procrastination makes excuses. Jonah was not willing to preach repentance in Nineveh. Even after he landed in the fish's belly, we know his heart was not truly willing because of his attitude. In Luke 9:59–62 we read some telling verses for procrastinators to meditate on:

He said to another man, "Follow Me." But he said, "Lord, let me first go and bury my father." Jesus said to him, "Leave the dead to bury their own dead. But you go and preach the kingdom of God." Yet another said, "Lord, I will follow You, but let me first go bid farewell to those at my house." Jesus said to him, "No one who puts his hand to the plow and looks back at things is fit for the kingdom of God."

✓ Examine your attitude toward the Lord's assignments and commands toward you. Are you ready to move ahead with joy? Do you delight to do His will? Or do you resent it? Do you have a bad attitude? Ask the Lord to help you get your attitude in line with His will.

✓ If you just cannot make yourself willing, ask the Lord to make you willing to be willing. Pray according to Psalm 110:3 (KJV), "Thy people shall be willing in the day of thy power."

✓ Actively surrender your will to the Lord. Do it over and over and over again if you have to, declaring war on your flesh, your soulish desires and enemy temptations.

✓ Cultivate a healthy fear of the Lord in your life. Study the many verses Proverbs offers about the benefits of the fear of the Lord.

In the next chapter we will deal with pride. Your flesh will be tempted to skip this chapter, but know this: Without humility, not only will you miss your next-level opportunity, you could find yourself demoted among your peers.

5

Humility: The Prophet's Equalizer

For My hand made all those things, thus all those things have come to be, says the LORD. But to this man I will look, even to him who is poor and of a contrite spirit, and trembles at My word.

Isaiah 66:2

When the Lord first called me into prophetic ministry, one of the elder prophets in the church asked my best friend how I was taking it. In other words, there was a legitimate concern that I might rise up in pride, thinking I was better than every other believer, like so many young prophets do.

There was much intercession over my life—probably far more than I even know—as I grappled with this high calling, the warfare that goes along with it and, yes, the temptation toward prophetic pride. After all, knowledge puffs up, or as the Modern English Version translates it, "knowledge produces arrogance" (1 Corinthians 8:1).

It is vital that the prophet guard his heart from pride because it perverts the prophetic voice. Entire books have been penned on humility, and if you are a prophet you should keep a few of them in your library and read through them regularly. Andrew Murray's classic *Humility* should be on every prophet's shelf. Another good one is R. T. Kendall's *The Power of Humility*. The truth of the matter is that apart from Him we "can do nothing" (John 15:5). We can see nothing. We can speak nothing. We can say nothing. We need to be utterly dependent on Him. That is true for every believer, but how much more for His prophets. How much more for the mouthpiece of God. If we do not stand in the counsel of the Lord to see or hear His word, we do not have anything to say (Jeremiah 23:18). And if we have something to say, it is not because we are more spiritual than anyone else—it is because He gave it to us.

I call humility the prophet's equalizer because it causes us not to think more highly of ourselves than we ought (see Romans 12:3). Humility encourages us to count others more significant than ourselves (see Philippians 2:3). Humility allows us to receive the grace we need to walk in prophetic ministry (see James 4:6).

I believe a key to the Third Great Awakening is humble prophets who will lead God's people into repentance. The only question is, Will you be one of them? Are you willing to be a nameless, faceless prophet who cares more about God's glory than your own? Will you be that unsung prophet?

The Unsung Prophet

Paul Revere gets plenty of glory for his role in the American Revolution. Our history books depict the emboldened Bostonian straddling his horse as he rides furiously to warn Samuel Adams and John Hancock that British troops were marching to arrest them. We have seen paintings depicting his famed midnight ride, heard songs commemorating his selfless bravery and read literature that heralds the adventure behind his proclamation that "the British are coming!"

Revere certainly deserves recognition for his brave acts of patriotism, but he hardly acted alone. In fact, there were many unsung heroes who we do not hear about, like William Dawes. Dawes was also commissioned to deliver the message about the impending arrival of enemy troops and met up with Revere in Lexington. Dawes's act was just as heroic, but we do not sing songs or write poetry about him. Revere borrowed a horse from his friend Deacon John Larkin for the historic journey, but few have ever heard his name.

Indeed, there are many unsung heroes of the American Revolution, faithful men and women who were dedicated to reformation. They were not concerned about their own glory. They were acting for the glory of the Creator to establish one nation under God, indivisible, with liberty and justice for all. Today we are at the front end of another revolution, a spiritual revolution that seeks to establish one Kingdom under God, indivisible, with liberty and justice for all.

Sure, there will be Paul Revere prophets who announce critical messages for the hour in the national spotlight. But there will be many more whose names we will never know—but who are just as instrumental in bringing God's will to earth as it is in heaven. I call them the unsung prophets. They are the faithful mouthpieces of God who complete their assignment without the demand for personal recognition and fanfare. They are the prophetic heroes who bring change to their generation by being obedient to the Spirit of God.

That may mean delivering a message that promotes another believer while you remain in relative obscurity. It may mean tireless watches on the wall while others are prophesying on the circuit. Or it may mean a behind-the-scenes wrestling match with principalities and powers to make a way for others to preach the Gospel of the Kingdom. The common characteristic of these unsung prophets is self-sacrifice. These prophetic heroes are not seeking their own honor—complete with titles, radio shows and conference invitations—they are seeking to honor the One who commissioned them.

Which Prophet Anointed Jehu?

Remember when Jehu was anointed King of Israel? Can you tell me who anointed him? You cannot remember, can you? That is because the Bible does not record the name of the prophet who accepted this important assignment.

> The prophet Elisha summoned a man from the company of the prophets and said to him, "Tuck your cloak into your belt, take this flask of olive oil with you and go to Ramoth Gilead. When you get there, look for Jehu son of Jehoshaphat, the son of Nimshi. Go to him, get him away from his companions and take him into an inner room. Then take the flask and pour the oil on his head and declare, "This is what the LORD says: I anoint you king over Israel." Then open the door and run; don't delay!
>
> 2 Kings 9:1–3 NIV

This unnamed prophet obeyed Elisha's command. He sought out Jehu, anointed him as king over Israel and commissioned him to destroy the house of Ahab. This unnamed prophet went on to deliver a powerful prophetic word about the fate of Jezebel—dogs would devour her in Jezreel—and then he opened the door and ran, giving no one an opportunity to applaud his powerful prophetic announcement or pat him on the back for a job well done.

> So he arose, went into the house, poured the oil on his head, and said to him, "Thus says the LORD, God of Israel: I am anointing you king over the people of the LORD, over Israel.

You will strike the house of Ahab your master, and I will avenge the blood of my servants the prophets and the blood of all the servants of the LORD from the hand of Jezebel. The whole house of Ahab will perish, and I will cut off from Ahab all the males in Israel, both imprisoned and free. I will make the house of Ahab like the house of Jeroboam son of Nebat and like the house of Baasha the son of Ahijah. Dogs will eat Jezebel in the territory of Jezreel, and no one will bury her." Then he opened the door and fled.

2 Kings 9:6–10

Jehu would ride his chariot furiously to Jezreel. Jezebel's fate was just as the unnamed prophet had announced. Jehu gets all the recognition, but it was the unsung prophet's faithfulness to complete his mission that marked a major turning point for Israel.

Whose Honor Are You Seeking?

There are other examples of unnamed prophets who accomplished important works in the Bible, and there are hundreds of modern-day prophets following in those humble footsteps. Thank God for the prophets who seek to honor the One who sent them instead of vying for self-glorification.

I have heard unappreciated prophets mutter about how "prophets [are] not without honor except in [their] own country" (Matthew 13:57). It is true that local congregations should treat their prophetic gifts with respect. It is true that if they believe the prophets they will prosper (see 2 Chronicles 20:20). It is true that God does not take kindly to those who touch His anointed and do His prophets harm (see Psalm 105:15). But that does not mean the prophet should don a bad attitude when his prophetic word is not received or get offended when someone forgets to address him with his ministry gift title.

Let me take you on a quick bunny trail that will help you if you struggle when people reject your prophetic utterances. Do not take the rejection personally. If you are delivering a true word from the Lord, the people are not rejecting you. They are rejecting the word of the Lord. That was the case with Samuel. Consider Samuel's prophetic reputation: "And Samuel grew, and the LORD was with him and did not let any of his words fall to the ground. All Israel from Dan even to Beersheba knew that Samuel was proven to be a prophet of the LORD" (1 Samuel 3:19–20).

Nevertheless, Saul did not receive Samuel's prophetic word. Samuel told Saul:

> The LORD sent me to anoint you king over His people, over Israel. Now therefore, heed the voice of the words of the LORD. Thus says the LORD of hosts: "I will punish Amalek for what he did to Israel, how he ambushed him on the way when he came up from Egypt. Now go and attack Amalek, and utterly destroy all that they have, and do not spare them. But kill both man and woman, infant and nursing child, ox and sheep, camel and donkey."
>
> 1 Samuel 15:1–3 NKJV

Again, Saul did not receive Samuel's prophetic word—not because it was false. Not because it bred fear. Not because it was seeking to control. But because Saul was self-willed. Saul fulfilled part of the prophecy. He waged war against the Amalekites, but he did not utterly destroy everything. Saul "spared Agag and the best of the sheep, the oxen, the fatlings, the lambs, and all that was good, and were unwilling to utterly destroy them. But everything despised and worthless, that they utterly destroyed" (verse 9 NKJV).

And if the person rejects the word—or rejects you—do not respond in kind. Instead, go into intercession for them. This is the spirit of a true prophet. This is the spirit Samuel demonstrated: "Samuel went to Ramah, and Saul went up to his house at Gibeah of Saul. And Samuel went no more to see Saul until the day of his death. Nevertheless Samuel mourned for Saul" (verses 34–35 NKJV). True prophets have a mercy gift and are intercessors. When folks reject the prophetic word you deliver, remember Samuel. Amen.

Yes, it was Jesus who said, "A prophet is not without honor, except in his own country" (Mark 6:4). But are we seeking our own honor, or are we seeking to honor the Prophet? If we are seeking our own honor, we can expect little more than humiliation. If we are seeking to honor the Father, then we can expect to be exalted in due time as trusted vessels, fit for the Master's use.

Like William Dawes, we may not wind up in history books or even featured on Christian television and magazines, but we can rest assured that if we do the will of God as He establishes this spiritual revolution, we can be history makers in God's book. Instead of the fifteen minutes of fame that the world offers, we can enjoy the satisfaction that lasts for an eternity.

Humble Yourself under the Mighty Hand of God

I am sure you have heard stories about the humiliation that prophets go through. It used to scare me when I heard people tell stories about the humiliation they endured, but when you are going through it you realize that it is breaking you so He can make you.

If we get proactive about humbling ourselves under the mighty hand of God, He will not have to step in with circumstances that deal with the pride in our hearts nearly as much. We can cooperate with God, who gives grace to the humble, and have a much easier road. Of course, humiliation brings suffering to our flesh, so whether we humble ourselves or God arranges the humiliation for us, we are going to suffer.

The Bible clearly points to "the prophets, who spoke in the name of the Lord, as an example of suffering and patience" (James 5:10). When you think you have it bad, think about Isaiah taking off all his clothes and wandering around naked (see Isaiah 20). That must have been pretty humiliating. What about Jeremiah, who hid his underwear in a rock and after a long time went back for it (see Jeremiah 13)? Hosea married a prostitute and named their daughter Lo-Ruhamah, which means one who is "not loved" (Hosea 1:6 NIV). And we already talked about all the humiliating and strange prophetic acts Ezekiel completed. Let's not forget Jesus naked on the cross.

Matthew Henry makes this observation in his commentary on James 5:

> The prophets, on whom God put the greatest honour, and for whom he had the greatest favour, were most afflicted: and, when we think that the best men have had the hardest usage in this world, we should hereby be reconciled to affliction. Observe further, Those who were the greatest examples of suffering affliction were also the best and greatest examples of patience: tribulation worketh patience. Hereupon James gives it to us as the common sense of the faithful (v. 11): We count those happy who endure: we look upon righteous and patient sufferers as the happiest people.[1]

These prophets of whom James and Henry wrote suffered to do the will of God, setting aside their own ambitions and pride. The word *suffering* refers to hardship. That could be financial problems or health problems or some other trial. Trials purify our faith, and they also cultivate humility in our hearts and position us in a place where we learn to hear the voice of the Lord even more clearly because of our desperation. Indeed, Abraham Lincoln is said to have put it this way: "I have been driven many times upon my knees by the overwhelming conviction that I had nowhere else to go. My own wisdom and that of all about me seemed insufficient for that day."

The Making of a Prophetic Prima Donna

In my editorial role at *Charisma* magazine I came across all kinds. There are many among the nameless, faceless generation who walk in a level of humility and honor that I aspire to. Then there are apostolic abusers and prophetic prima donnas, divas and all-out "exalted prophetesses" who walk in pride and pretense and do not seem to care who knows it.

One encounter with a prophetic prima donna got me thinking: How do Christians with international ministries, book deals and large staffs become such drama queens (and kings) who think more highly of themselves than they ought? Did they start their journey as part of the nameless, faceless generation, only to fall victim to pride's puffery? Or were they always secretly striving for the spotlight? Were they always willing to climb over (and even trample on) anyone and everyone to get to the top of the ministry ladder?

What causes some Christians to flat out abuse the people around them once they "arrive" in a position of authority? What does the making of a prophetic prima donna look like? How does it happen? And how can we keep from falling into this trap as God promotes us to more visible roles in the Kingdom or in society?

Yes, I have a lot of questions because I do not want to become an apostolic abuser who maligns the character of others to cover up my own shortcomings. I do not want to turn into a demanding prophetic prima donna who is too big for her own britches.

In fact, every time I run into one of these prophetic prima donnas, I walk away with the fear of God in me because I know that anyone can be deceived by the pride of life—especially when success keeps knocking louder and louder, and especially when no one is willing to hold you accountable for the pattern of pride that consistently manifests in your life.

It seems the Hollywood Christianity syndrome causes even the most discerning believers to turn a blind eye to the evidence of deep character flaws that could be a symptom of serious sin. If we cannot rightly discern and lovingly deal with the visible pride of apostolic abusers and prophetic prima donnas, how will we avoid the even greater deceptions coming in the end times?

After much prayer and reflection, I have come to this conclusion: There is not any one formula for the making of a prophetic prima donna. I think we can fall into pride any number of ways. After all, we will have layers of pride to peel away so long as we live in these fleshly tents.

Think about it for a minute. From the world's standards, these prophetic prima donnas have plenty of which to be proud. "Successful" ministers have worked hard to get where they are. They sacrificed a lot. We should honor them in a godly way for laboring over the Word in prayer and in service to the Body.

But I believe the snare of the pride of life becomes a dangerous reality when people begin to idolize "successful" ministers as demigods who are above reproach. We have seen this time and time again when congregants vehemently defend and refuse to believe even the most blatant and public sins of their pastors. But it is just as real in the local church with unapproachable pastors.

Too often, these ministers are surrounded by yes men who are either too scared or too ambitious to tell the pastor his behavior is not Christlike. Instead of speaking the truth in love, they pray in silence. But too often nothing changes because the deception is so great.

Let me be clear: I am not giving anyone a license to rebuke your pastor or anyone else. I am merely suggesting that perhaps some leaders would not fall if those whom the Holy Spirit quickened to speak the truth in love obeyed His prompting.

With all that said, I am quite sure we all need to get over ourselves. We cannot sit idly by and point the finger at the apostolic abusers and prophetic prima donnas at the expense of peeling the onion of pride in our own lives. The truth is, we are probably all too proud to see just how much pride we really walk in, and if we do not think we have pride in our souls, then we are already deceived.

I have come to the conclusion that in order to avoid falling into the sins of the apostolic abusers and prophetic prima donnas—the ones who mistreat people and begin to think they deserve a measure of the glory for running the ministry the Lord assigned them—we need to frequently check our own hearts. And we need to be open to hear those who labor with us if they suggest we may have an issue to deal with.

We need to ask ourselves, How are we treating people? How do we think about people? Do we take God's glory? Walk in false humility? I think if we all focused on walking in humility and love, we would be more ready to hear and obey the Holy Spirit to help others whose pride may be setting them up for a fall.

Mother Teresa offered us a few ways we can practice humility:

To speak as little as possible of one's self. To mind one's own business. Not to want to manage other people's affairs. To avoid curiosity. To accept contradictions and correction cheerfully. To pass over the mistakes of others. To accept insults and injuries. To accept being slighted, forgotten and disliked. To be kind and gentle even under provocation. Never to stand on one's dignity. To choose always the hardest.[2]

We would all do well to follow this advice from one of the meekest women on earth. It echoes principles in the Bible, such as, "Let another man praise you, and not your own mouth; a stranger, and not your own lips" (Proverbs 27:2), as well as Christ's Sermon on the Mount (see Matthew 5–7).

Waging War on Misguided Motives

I do not expect this chapter to be among the most popular I have ever written. In fact, if you are looking for prophetic insight into the latest trends in spiritual warfare, you may as well stop reading. But if you are interested in touching God's heart now and heaping up eternal recompense, then join me in pursuing the rewards of obscurity.

In the Sermon on the Mount, Jesus outlined three specific areas in which we are tempted to put on a show for man: giving, praying and fasting. Giving, praying and fasting should be motivated by love and an obedient pursuit of His will that comes out of that love. When we give, pray and fast with the right motive, we can be sure rewards are waiting.

On the other hand, making a show of giving, praying and fasting ultimately backfires. Rather than love and an obedient pursuit of His will that comes out of that love, people who put on a show have their reward in full. That reward is called the recognition and admiration of man. I do not know about you, but I would rather receive God's slight nod over man's standing ovation. And you get more than God's slight nod when His Kingdom purposes motivate your heart.

In Matthew 6:1–4 (NKJV), Jesus said:

> Take heed that you do not do your charitable deeds before men, to be seen by them. Otherwise you have no reward from your Father in heaven. Therefore, when you do a charitable deed, do not sound a trumpet before you as the hypocrites do in the synagogues and in the streets, that they may have glory from men. Assuredly, I say to you, they have their reward. But when you do a charitable deed, do not let your left hand know what your right hand is doing, that your charitable deed may be in secret; and your Father who sees in secret will Himself reward you openly.

Can you imagine? The religious leaders of the day—Jesus called them hypocrites—actually sounded a trumpet to draw attention to their good deeds. Their motive was clearly to look like the hotshots of Israel. And despite how deeply they dug into their pockets, the only reward they would ever get was the attention of man. God wants no part in that pretense. The one poor widow who is willing to throw two mites quietly into the offering touches the Father's heart more than every attention-seeking religious spirit put together (see Mark 12:41–47).

The Attention-Seeking Prayer Warrior

Jesus then said this:

> And when you pray, you shall not be like the hypocrites. For they love to pray standing in the synagogues and on the corners of the streets, that they may be seen by men. Assuredly, I say to you, they have their reward. But you, when you pray, go into your room, and when you have shut your door, pray to your Father who is in the secret place; and your Father who sees in secret will reward you openly.
>
> Matthew 6:5–6 NKJV

Once again, Jesus pointed out the hypocrites. Their motive is to be seen by men, and they have their reward through those who marvel at their dedication to prayer. Or maybe their motive is to demonstrate their ability to shout the devil down louder than their neighbor so they can prove what a fierce spiritual warrior they really are.

I have always wondered what kinds of prayers the pharisaical hypocrites prayed. Maybe it sounded something like this: "God, I thank You that I am not like other men—extortioners, unjust, adulterers, or even as this tax collector. I fast twice a week; I give tithes of all that I possess" (Luke 18:11–12 NKJV). There is nothing wrong with praying in public; it is the motivation that matters. God much prefers the one who cries for mercy.

Finally, Jesus said:

> Moreover, when you fast, do not be like the hypocrites, with a sad countenance. For they disfigure their faces that they may appear to men to be fasting. Assuredly, I say to you, they have their reward. But you, when you fast, anoint your head and wash your face, so that you do not appear to men to be fasting, but to your Father who is in the secret place; and your Father who sees in secret will reward you openly.
>
> Matthew 6:16–18 NKJV

Every year, we see ministries call fasts. And that is an awesome thing. There is flesh-killing power in fasting. But if we are motivated by putting our name on the church's fasting list so others can see how we are starving ourselves for the cause, then our motives are all wrong. How ironic that even in fasting some have fleshly rather than godly motives.

I Am Not Trying to Impress You

Beyond giving, fasting and praying, people do all sorts of things to look more spiritual, more humble, more "whatever" than the other guy. The point is this: When you do things to impress people, you have your reward. Even if you start off in obedience to God by giving away your most prized possession, if you make a big deal about it—if you make sure everyone knows what you did so you can look like a sacrificial giver—you have your reward in full.

We should ultimately be motivated by eternity. When we look at our actions through an eternal lens, we see what really matters and what really does not. When we behave as if an eternal God is watching—and He is—then we become aware of what truly matters and what truly does not in this life.

The rewards of man may feel good in the moment, but even man's greatest rewards are fleeting. Ultimately, only God's rewards can truly satisfy our hearts. That is why I choose to pursue the rewards of obscurity. Anything that is not motivated by love will not last in eternity.

Next-Level Prophetic Exercises

The Bible tells us "knowledge puffs up" (1 Corinthians 8:1 NKJV). Prophets, by gifting, walk in revelatory knowledge. Pride can creep in at any level to bring a great fall. It is important to maintain humility at every level and continue cultivating more and more humility as you climb higher in your gifting. Take some time to work through these exercises.

- ✓ Do you have a haughty attitude? Do you think more highly of yourself than you ought? Inspired by the Holy Spirit, Paul warned against this attitude (see Romans 12:3). Ask the Holy Spirit to show you any areas of your life where you may feel superior, then ask Him to help you embrace humility.
- ✓ Do you get ruffled when someone does not acknowledge your title? Or do you crave a title? That is a sign of pride. Ask the Lord to make you like the unsung prophet.
- ✓ Do you seek attention for your ministry? Feel the need to prove yourself? That is a sign of rejection or pride. Ask God to deliver you from these voices.
- ✓ Read books on humility. I recommended Andrew Murray's classic book *Humility* in this chapter. I have read it many times and have given away almost every copy I purchased to people I mentor. The truths in the book are that vital for prophetic people.
- ✓ Ask the Lord for the grace of humility so you can obey the command to humble yourself. God never commands us to do anything without giving us the grace to do it.

✓ Study the humility of Christ, including passages like Philippians 2:6–8, which speaks of Jesus this way:

> Who, being in the form of God, did not consider equality with God something to be grasped. But He emptied Himself, taking upon Himself the form of a servant, and was made in the likeness of men. And being found in the form of a man, He humbled Himself and became obedient to death, even death on a cross.

In the next chapter, we explore selflessness, which is a fruit of humility that should run deep through the prophet's heart.

6

Selflessness: The Prophet's Quest

> Nor do I count my life of value to myself, so that
> I may joyfully finish my course and the ministry
> which I have received from the Lord Jesus, to testify
> to the gospel of the grace of God.
>
> Acts 20:24

The Holy Spirit is a practical Teacher. He does not always choose to send an angel or a prophet to declare His will for our lives. Nor does He always speak to us in a still, small voice. No, sometimes the Lord sends loud and clear messages through our natural surroundings. It is up to us to remain sensitive enough to the Spirit to see prophetic implications in everyday life.

Indeed, remaining sensitive to the Holy Spirit offers us the ultimate navigational system. You will never wind up taking a dangerous detour off the prophetic highway if you stay tuned to your supernatural Global Positioning Satellite (GPS) system. It is more accurate than any twenty-first-century technology, and it never fails to show you where you need to go and exactly how to get there, albeit often one faith-filled step at a time. You just have to remember to flip the switch, so to speak, as you set your mind on the things of the Spirit instead of on the things of the flesh.

I am accustomed to the Holy Ghost speaking to me through the illumination of natural events that correspond to spiritual truths. Do not get me wrong. I do not look for deep prophetic directives if I lose a button on my blouse. (You can get goofy in a hurry if you try to tie the voice of God to anything and everything.) But I do try to remain aware of the Holy Spirit's presence and ask Him if there is significance to people, places or objects that strike my spirit. I am sure you do the same.

On one such instance I was driving down Interstate 95 coming into Fort Lauderdale. I saw a row of orange garage-like doors that I had seen many times before in passing. This time the colors seemed bolder and more vibrant, almost glowing. I do not remember the brand name of the facility, but I do remember a key term on that sign: self-storage. I continued to drive down the highway with a *hmm* floating around in my soul. Suddenly a sign above a row of blue doors with that same term—self-storage—demanded my attention.

"Okay, God. What's up?" I asked, certain I was about to miss an important lesson if I failed to inquire at His temple. Well, it does not take a prophet to interpret the message. It was clearer than 20/20 vision. It was time to put my *self* in storage. It was time to decrease a little more, that He might increase (see John 3:30). It was time to exchange the heavy weight of self-will for self-sacrifice. It was time to go to a new level.

Maybe you have been there. You are frustrated because you know the prophetic gift of God inside you should be producing more. After all, you have read the books, you have gone to the prayer meetings and you have even plugged in to the work of the ministry. Yet you feel more like a stagnant reservoir than a free-flowing river. Of course, there could be many different reasons why your breakthrough has not manifested. But will you, just for a moment, entertain the notion that it could have something to do with your *self*?

There is something I call the self-willed syndrome that I can share with you for a good reason: I have lived with it and learned to recognize its onset. While we all have our own will, we have a choice of how we will use it. When we align ourselves with God's will, all is well with us. It is only when we start trumpeting the "What about me?" song that we become aware of the potentially deadly group of signs and symptoms that reveal our sickly spiritual condition.

What we are about to find out is that *self* can not only hold you back from the next level of your prophetic ministry, but it also can hold you back from entering the Kingdom of God.

Self This, Self That and Self the Other

The dictionary has a laundry list of definitions that begin with *self*. Most of them are self-serving. There is *self-absorption*, *self-advancement*, *self-appointed*. And we have not even gotten out of the As yet. There is *self-deception*, *self-existent* and *self-government*. There is *self-indulgence*, *self-justification* and *self-reliance*. Oh, let's not forget *self-righteousness*, that religious version that looks good on the outside but is rotten on the inside. Get the picture? (Perhaps that is why the Lord showed me a row of doors—one self-storage unit for each of the "self" areas I needed to put away.)

All that said, I believe the very worst *self* issue is self-will. A self-willed person is stubborn about getting his or her own way. A self-willed person is a willful person. The willful person does what he or she pleases. The only problem is when what he or she pleases does not please God. That is when self-will takes us down the path of self-government, past the alley of self-indulgence and toward the path of self-deception.

The Bible, for example, says that a bishop must not be self-willed (see Titus 1:7). How much more a prophet who is supposed to be a mouthpiece of God. The prophet must serve the will of God at all costs. It does not always make sense to our souls, but it is not our job to figure out God's grand plan. It is our job to help fulfill it.

Hosea tells the story of Ephraim, who "played the prostitute" (Hosea 5:3 AMP). Hosea explains, "Ephraim is oppressed, crushed in judgment, because in selfwill he walked after the commandment [of man]" (Hosea 5:11 DARBY). And the apostle Peter mentions a group that walks after the lusts of the flesh and describes them as self-willed (see 2 Peter 2:10 DARBY). He calls this group "spots and blemishes" (verse 13 DARBY). He says they are deceitful and will receive the wages of unrighteousness. That is not exactly the company I want to keep, but you know what they say: Birds of a feather flock together.

Have We Not Prophesied in Your Name?

Now let's bring this home. Self-will is one ingredient in the recipe for a false prophet. How can I say that? I do not have to. Jesus said it for me, and Matthew recorded it in his gospel. In Matthew 7:15 Jesus tells us to "beware of false prophets" who appear as harmless as sheep but are as dangerous as wolves. Then in verse 21 Jesus goes on to warn the disciples that not everyone who says "Lord, Lord" will enter into the Kingdom of heaven. Jesus makes it crystal clear that only those who do the will of the Father will enter in.

> Many will say to me in that day, Lord, Lord, have we not prophesied in thy name? and in thy name have cast out devils? and in thy name done many wonderful works? And then will I profess unto them, I never knew you: depart from me, ye that work iniquity.
>
> Matthew 7:22–23 KJV

So what are we going to do with that? Jesus undeniably calls out those who prophesy, cast out devils and do mighty works. He is obviously talking about prophetic ministry in these verses (not that they do not apply to anyone else). Jesus began His teaching with a warning about false prophets and then drilled down to the core issue of some false prophets: self-will.

Let's look at this verse again in light of other translations of the Greek words. *Prophesied* translates as "exercised the prophetic office." *Name* translates as "authority." *Wonderful works* translates as "miracles." *Knew* translates as "allowed." And *iniquity* translates as "lawlessness." So the verses could read this way:

> Many will say to me in that day, "Lord, Lord, have we not *exercised the prophetic office* by your *authority*? And by your *authority* cast out devils? And by your *authority* done many miracles?" And I will profess unto them, "I never *allowed* you: depart from me, ye that work *lawlessness*."

In other words, "You did not do the will of My Father. You did your own will. You were self-willed. You did what you wanted to do without asking God what He thought about it. You prophesied without permission. You cast out devils to draw attention to yourself. You used your gifts, which are without repentance, as it pleased you. You may have used My name, but I didn't call *you* to do those things."

Making It Prophetically Plain

Let me hit this self-willed devil right out of the ballpark with *The Message* Bible translation:

> I can see it now—at the Final Judgment thousands strutting up to me and saying, "Master, we preached the Message, we bashed the demons, our God-sponsored projects had everyone

talking." And do you know what I am going to say? "You missed the boat. All you did was use me to make yourselves important. You don't impress me one bit. You're out of here."

Matthew 7:22–23 MESSAGE

I do not know about you, but that was enough to drive me to the self-storage facility and pay the price to rent as many units as it would take to unload self-assertion, self-conceit, self-interest—and self-will.

It is a character issue. Jesus said we would know people by their fruit. But looking at the fruit of a ministry is not enough. We must look at character, which should be ever-ripening without rotting.

Think about Jesus, the Prophet. He is our prototype, and it is His testimony we speak when we prophesy. Jesus did not seek His own will. He sought the will of the Father who sent Him (see John 6:38). Doubtless, being committed to the will of the Father was much easier for Him when He was casting out devils and prophesying, but He stuck to His guns even to the point of blood.

You remember the episode in the Garden of Gethsemane. The hour of His betrayal was at hand. He admitted to Peter and the two sons of Zebedee that His soul was exceedingly sorrowful, even to death. He asked God to spare Him the pain of the cross and His subsequent separation from the King of glory three times, but each time Jesus ended His prayer with the same essential words: "Not my will but yours be done" (see Matthew 26:42).

Pick Up Your Cross and Follow Him

Jesus understands it is not always easy to put down our own wills to do the will of the Father, and He has given us the power of the Holy Spirit to help us take up our cross and follow His

example. I like the way the Amplified Bible puts it. After Jesus
had just rebuked Peter, saying, "Get behind Me, Satan!" because
He was trying to talk Jesus out of going to the cross, Jesus then
used it as a teaching example:

> For you do not have a mind intent on promoting what God wills,
> but what pleases men [you are not on God's side, but that of
> men]. And Jesus called [to Him] the throng with His disciples
> and said to them, If anyone intends to come after Me, let him
> deny himself [forget, ignore, disown, and lose sight of himself
> and his own interests] and take up his cross, and [joining Me as
> a disciple and siding with My party] follow with Me [continu-
> ally, cleaving steadfastly to Me].
>
> Mark 8:33–36 AMPC

In his book *Purifying the Prophetic*, R. Loren Sandford offers a sign of the times and calls for Christians to recall the
Lord's words in Matthew 16:24–25 (NASB): "If anyone wishes
to come after Me, he must deny himself, and take up his cross
and follow Me. For whoever wishes to save his life will lose it;
but whoever loses his life for My sake will find it." With clear
prophetic urgency Sandford writes:

> Self-focus is killing us. We are losing our lives, but for all the
> wrong reasons—not for the Lord's sake, but for the pursuit of
> self. Self-absorption has become so much a part of our culture,
> and we have become so accustomed to it, that it has come to
> feel completely natural to us. We fail to see how deeply we have
> been captivated by it and have become unaware of how much
> we have lost.[1]

Prophets and prophetic people, maybe you are like me and
have seen the same self-storage sign. I challenge you not to
flow in spiritual gifts without exercising self-control, self-denial
and self-discipline. I appeal to you to go through some self-
examination, self-restraint and self-revealing. Rid yourself of

self-will. Self-will is stubbornness, and "stubbornness is as iniquity and idolatry" (1 Samuel 15:23). The road to self-deception is not as long as you might think. And the end is self-destruction. Let's continually visit the self-storage facility and off-load all that is unpleasing to God so that we can give our entire will to the Lord Almighty.

Now is the time for us to lay aside childish ways and adopt His ways for His glory. Now is the time for us to surrender with all our heart, with all our soul, with all our strength and with all our mind to the will of God—even at the expense of our personal ambitions, hopes and plans. It is time to lay everything on the altar and let the Lord give back only that which agrees with His plans and purposes.

Just like Jesus told the woman at the well in the Valley of Shechem, God is Spirit, and His worshipers "must worship Him in spirit and truth" (John 4:24). So choose this day whom you will serve: self or Spirit. I urge you by the Spirit of God not to be "conformed to this world, but be transformed by the renewing of your mind, that you may prove what is the good and acceptable and perfect will of God" to a lost and dying world (Romans 12:2). And I pray that "you may be filled with the knowledge of His will in all wisdom and spiritual understanding"—and that you may be "strengthened with all might according to His glorious power" to obey the will of God in all things (Colossians 1:9, 11).

Letting Go of Your Right to Be Understood

Prophets have a longing to be understood—but are often misunderstood. It seems I have been misunderstood my whole life. I was an extremely shy kid, but some thought I was just a snob. Fast-forward a few years, and I embraced blue hair, black clothing—and more misunderstanding. As a prophetic voice, I am attacked, maligned and otherwise misunderstood on a weekly basis.

We have to remember that being misunderstood is a feeling that taps into the "self" to which we need to die. We *feel* misunderstood. But we may not be misunderstood at all. We could just feel that way because we do not get the response out of the person that we wanted.

Sometimes we need to accept misunderstandings and just let it be if we are going to move forward in relationships. If it is a trivial issue, we need to just let it pass. But that does not mean it does not cause us pain. There are a few different ways to handle real misunderstanding.

Get Over Your "Self"

The "misunderstood malady," as I call it, taps into self. It is our "self" that needs to feel understood. It is our "self" that feels rejected. It is our "self" that feels lonely. It is our "self" that gets depressed and wants to have a pity party. We need to get our minds off our self and on somebody else, helping others who are in much worse spots than we are. It is amazing how the burdens lift when you get your mind off yourself. And while you are helping someone else, God will help you.

Ultimately, when people misunderstand us, they are not trying to hurt us, so we should not get angry, resentful, bitter or unforgiving about it. Maybe they just cannot understand because they have not been in that place. But Jesus has.

The prophet Joseph could understand dreams, but nobody could understand him. His family misunderstood his motives (Genesis 37:4–10).

Joseph is an example of a young prophet who probably needed to keep his mouth shut about the call of God on his life. Family members rarely understand our calling unless they are on fire for the Lord. Remember, Jesus said a prophet is not without honor except in his hometown (see Mark 6:4). Joseph was so misunderstood that his brothers just got him out of the picture.

How did Joseph handle this? He kept doing the right thing even when the wrong thing was happening to him. I believe he carried that pain with him for the twenty-some-odd years that it took him to get from the pit to the palace. When his brothers came to Egypt and he finally revealed himself to them, he wept. It is possible that is when all those hurts and wounds came out.

Many times, if we are feeling misunderstood or rejected, we need to go ahead and have a good cry. But we do not cry in pity for ourselves. We cry and sob at the Lord's feet, asking Him to take the pain away from us, asking Him to heal our hearts, asking Him to help us to forgive.

Jesus was misunderstood—and it did not seem to bother His soul one bit. The Israelites were expecting a Messiah who would lead a natural army. Most people did not understand who Jesus really was or what His mission was. Even those closest to Him—His family and His friends—did not understand Him. His family thought He was off His rocker (see Mark 3:20–21). Before the cross, He was an embarrassment to His brethren. He was even accused of being demon-possessed (see Matthew 12:22–30).

Keep Speaking the Truth

How did Jesus respond to all of this? He just spoke the truth in love and kept on going. He persevered on His mission. He did not even take a time-out to go up to the mountain and pray all night. He just kept right on doing what He was called to do. His "nevertheless" attitude sought the will of God. Ultimately, millions would understand Him, but still many more do not.

Remember that Jesus understands you perfectly (see Hebrews 4:15). His understanding is inexhaustible and boundless (see Psalm 147:5). He is able immediately to run to the cry of those who are suffering (see Hebrews 2:18).

These are verses that will help you stay steady in the midst of the pain of misunderstanding and the persecution that sometimes goes along with it. Pray this: "Lord, I thank You that You understand me. I will not let my life be ruled by feelings. My happiness does not depend on other people understanding me. I am free from the misunderstood malady."

Get Your Mind off the Misunderstanding

Whether we face an honest misunderstanding or a nasty accusation, we need to respond correctly because the Lord is watching. He wants to make it right. He wants to vindicate us. So if you are misunderstood, here are some practical tips for getting your mind off the misunderstanding:

1. First, pray for those who misunderstand you.
2. Be kind and respectful toward those who slight you.
3. Seek the good of those who judge you wrongly.
4. Protect the reputation of those who slander you.
5. Privately work in the best interests of those who are working against you, and purposely avoid telling them what you do for them.
6. Thank the Lord for the purifying effect it has on your life when you are misunderstood.

When we do these things, we have the Spirit of Jesus, "who, when He was reviled, did not revile in return; when He suffered, He did not threaten, but committed Himself to Him who judges righteously" (1 Peter 2:23 NKJV).

Next-Level Prophetic Exercises

Selfishness is a stumbling block. It will cause you to miss your next-level prophetic advancement because the true prophet's ministry is a selfless ministry. Like any gift or office, the anointing you carry is not to serve yourself or your goals. The prophetic anointing on your life is to be distributed selflessly, for the good of others.

✓ Do you have selfish attitudes? Do not answer too quickly. Ask the Holy Spirit to reveal any selfish attitudes. If He shows you something, be quick to repent.

✓ Attack the selfishness in your heart by meditating on verses such as Philippians 2:4; 2 Timothy 3:2–4; 1 John 3:17; 1 Corinthians 10:24 and Galatians 6:2.

✓ Consider the selflessness of God in verses such as John 3:16; Ephesians 5:25 and Galatians 5:22–24.

✓ Ask the Lord to help you crucify your selfishness and deny yourself and your own desires in order to pick up your cross and follow Christ (see Luke 9:23).

In the next chapter, we explore prophets and prayer. Prayer is the gateway to your next level.

7

Prayer: The Prophet's Gateway

> But if they are prophets, and if the word of the
> LORD is with them, let them now make intercession
> to the LORD of Hosts.
>
> Jeremiah 27:18

Are you building walls of religion or towers of prayer? Your answer could denote the difference between a woe-filled fate and a fulfilled destiny.

Prophets obsessed by the fear of man or unholy desires will not fulfill God's ultimate plan, much less make it to the next level. We must be careful, then, not to prophesy according to the party line in order to establish and preserve popularity in ministry circuits. If we fall into this trap, we find ourselves in danger of perverting the gift of God by building walls of religion.

True prophets are not always the most popular fivefold ministers on the block because they are bold enough to release a word of the Lord that deals with sin or that warns the local church of potentially unpleasant circumstances coming down the proverbial pike. In order to properly carry this mantle, genuine prophets must build towers of prayer.

False prophets build walls of religion that lead people astray with fabricated edification, misleading exhortation and counterfeit comfort.

> These evil prophets deceive my people by saying, "All is peaceful" when there is no peace at all! It's as if the people have built a flimsy wall, and these prophets are trying to reinforce it by covering it with whitewash! Tell these whitewashers that their wall will soon fall down.
>
> Ezekiel 13:10–11 NLT

Verily, verily, the whitewashed walls of religion are going to come tumbling down in a heap of self-righteous rubble, and the false prophets are coming down right along with them. Let's not forget that Jesus pronounced woe on the pharisaical hypocrites, calling them "whitewashed tombs" that look beautiful on the outside but are "full of dead men's bones" and everything unclean (Matthew 23:27).

You cannot whitewash sin. You cannot whitewash religion. And you cannot whitewash false prophecy. We must guard our hearts in order to maintain a pure prophetic flow and a life of prayer that will wash away the plans of the enemy instead of fortifying his deception by watering down the truth for the sake of acceptance.

True prophets may not always have the flair, charisma or appeal of their false twins, but who said they are supposed to? Jeremiah was not the most popular prophet in his time, nor was Ezekiel in his days. John the Baptist had his head served up on a silver platter for warning the people of the looming decision between everlasting life and eternal hellfire. But they were the unadulterated mouthpieces of God. And so it should be.

Prayer Separates the True from the False

One of the key differences between the true and the false prophet is prayer. The Bible says the foolish prophets discussed in the thirteenth chapter of Ezekiel did not stand in the gap or make up a hedge for the house of Israel so that it could endure the battle. These diviners did not intercede in prayer to protect God's people.

True prophets, by contrast, may not win any popularity contests in the local church, but they will sacrifice to make intercession. Instead of building walls of religion, they build towers of prayer—watchtowers in the spirit that allow them to see the assignments coming against the local church. They take that revelation and use it as spiritual mortar to make up a hedge in prayer.

You cannot separate a prophet from prayer any more than you can separate evangelists from preaching the Gospel. The very first time you ever see the word *prophet* in the Bible, it is connected to prayer. In the book of Genesis when Abimelech took Abraham's wife, the Lord said, "Now return the man's wife, for he is a prophet, and he will pray for you and you will live" (Genesis 20:7 NIV). While not every intercessor is a prophet, every prophet is an intercessor.

Consider the prophets of old. They were often called watchmen: "I have set watchmen upon thy walls, O Jerusalem, which shall never hold their peace day nor night: ye that make mention of the LORD, keep not silence" (Isaiah 62:6 KJV). Scripture reveals three types of prophetic sentinels whose mission is to stand guard, keep watch and report what they see. We find Old Testament prophets on the walls, walking in the streets of the city and in the countryside.

Watchmen on the walls are positioned to see far distances in the spirit and discern whether friend or foe is approaching. The watchman gives word to those in authority so they can decide whether to sound an alarm of welcome or an alarm of war.

In today's local church, these watchmen help protect against enemy attacks. Every prophet is called to this post.

Prophets also have a clear role in evangelism as watchmen who protect Gospel-preaching efforts against the destructive work of principalities and powers that keep the lost from hearing the truth. Jeremiah 4:17 (NLT) relates to these prophets in the harvest fields: "'They surround Jerusalem like watchmen around a field, for my people have rebelled against me,' says the LORD." Prophets should be deployed on local church outreaches and international missions to watch, guard, pull down and destroy opposition to the Good News.

In Song of Songs 3:3 and 5:7 (NIV) we read that "the watchmen found me as they made their rounds." In today's times, this watchman is assigned to stand guard over the Body of Christ to see emerging problems. This is a larger responsibility that carries with it a heavier prayer burden and greater implications for the Church at large.

Watch and Pray

The point is, all who stand in the fivefold function of prophet should keep their spiritual binoculars around their neck and watch. But not just watch—watch and pray always. Anyone carrying a prophetic mantle needs to examine the fruit of his or her ministry closely. If we have prophesied peace unto popularity, then we need to repent. We need to trade in our whitewash for some spiritual mortar and start building towers of prayer that will bring genuine edification, authentic exhortation and legitimate comfort to God's people.

Let us not be foolish prophets who build our ministries on the sands of seduction for the sake of acceptance, because Jehovah promises that rain will pour from the heavens, hailstones will come hurtling down and violent winds will burst forth against those whitewashed walls (see Ezekiel 13:11–12). When it does, you will be exposed.

Instead, let us build our ministries on the Rock and prophesy the mind of Christ. That way, when the hurricanes of religion come against the local church, when Jezebel hurls her spiritual sleet at the sanctuary and when the winds of witchcraft blow against the walls, the foundation of our ministries and our local churches will be fortified to stand and withstand in the day of battle.

Discerning the Call to Prophetic Intercession

There is plenty of talk about prayer, prophetic intercession, standing in the gap, making up the hedge, prayer burdens and, of course, spiritual warfare. But how do we discern the call to prayer? How do we recognize a proverbial prayer burden?

These questions may seem simple, but far too many prophets and prophetic intercessors have come to me carrying burdens they thought were their own when in reality they were feeling the weight of oppression over a person or a city. I know how they feel. It took me some years to learn to accurately divide soul and spirit.

The turning point for me was during a mission trip to Nicaragua. I woke up feeling severely depressed for no apparent reason. I felt down and out, like giving up, throwing in the towel, calling it quits and running home to pull the covers over my head. It felt like my best friend had just died. I sat there for about twenty minutes trying to figure out what was wrong with me and crying out to God to help me escape these oppressive feelings.

As I persisted, I heard that still, small voice in my spirit saying, "Despondent. This is how the people of this nation feel. Pray." Despondence is a feeling of extreme discouragement, dejection or depression. Once the Lord gave me that insight,

I joined with others in a circle to pray against the oppression with "the weapons of our warfare," which "are not carnal, but mighty through God to the pulling down of strongholds" (2 Corinthians 10:4).

I will always remember that experience, as it was my introduction to burden-bearing for the Lord. Later, this was confirmed by the teachings of the late E. M. Bounds, who wrote a number of classics on prayer. In his book *The Reality of Prayer*, he wrote:

> We have in the Holy Spirit an illustration and an enabler of what this intercession is and ought to be. We are charged to supplicate in the Spirit and to pray in the Holy Spirit. We are reminded that the Holy Spirit "helpeth our infirmities," and that while intercession is an art of so divine and so high a nature that though we know not what to pray for as we ought, yet the Spirit teaches us this heavenly science, by making intercession in us "with groanings which cannot be uttered." How burdened these intercessions of the Holy Spirit! How profoundly he feels the world's sin, the world's woe, and the world's loss, and how deeply he sympathizes with the dire conditions, are seen in his groanings which are too deep for utterance and too sacred to be voiced by him. He inspires us to this most divine work of intercession, and his strength enables us to sigh unto God for the oppressed, the burdened and the distressed creation. The Holy Spirit helps us in many ways.
>
> How intense will be the intercessions of the saints who supplicate in the spirit! How vain and delusive and how utterly fruitless and inefficient are prayers without the Spirit![1]

All Prophets Are Intercessors

Prophets are intercessors. An intercessor pleads with God on behalf of another. We see Abraham, Moses, Daniel and other prophets in the Bible interceding—and bearing the burdens—of people throughout Scripture. Abraham made intercession for the King Abimelech, who had taken his wife and brought a curse on the wombs of the women in his land (Genesis 20:7). Moses interceded for the nation of Israel when the Lord wanted to destroy them (Deuteronomy 9:13–14).

Jesus, our prototype Prophet, prayed for His disciples while He walked the earth and made the ultimate act of intercession when He hung on a cross to pay the price for our sins. Although His work on the cross is finished, His work of intercession continues. Hebrews 7:25 tells us He always "lives to make intercession for them."

Prophets who do not make intercession should not be prophesying. I base this assertion on Jeremiah 27:18, "But if they are prophets, and if the word of the LORD is with them, let them now make intercession to the LORD of Hosts." My mantra is "If you don't pray, you don't have anything to say." Prophets are burden-bearers for the Lord.

Let it not be said of us what the Lord said to Ezekiel:

> And I sought a man among them who should build up the wall and stand in the gap before Me for the land, that I should not destroy it, but I found none. Therefore have I poured out My indignation upon them; I have consumed them with the fire of My wrath; their own way have I repaid [by bringing it] upon their own heads.
>
> Ezekiel 22:30–31 AMPC

Signs of Prayer Burdens

Prayer burdens can be difficult to discern. That is because we are a three-part being: spirit, soul and body (see 1 Thessalonians 5:23). Our spirit man connects directly to God, but sometimes our soul and our flesh can disrupt the flow. As Spirit-led beings, we learn to discern whether or not we are having a rough day and need some rest or we are carrying a prayer burden for the Lord.

We have to separate our emotional realm from the spirit realm. The enemy is a deceiver, and he wants you to think the emotions or stirrings you are feeling are you—that there is something wrong with you. Know this: We can be walking through one of the worst days of our life and be carrying an intercessory prayer burden for someone else at the same time. When we enter into burden-bearing for the Lord, oftentimes we receive more strength to work through our own problems. He rewards the selfless act of intercession.

To walk accurately in the spirit, we have to train our spiritual senses to distinguish between our own discouragement and the Spirit's urgency to pray for someone else battling hopelessness. Are we oppressed because we are oppressed, or are we sensing oppression in the spiritual atmosphere so that we can stand in the gap? Both scenarios require prayer, but one is a petition to God on our own behalf, and the other is intercession, or burden-bearing, for another.

So how do you know if it is you or a prayer burden or there is something going on in your own soul? Typically, there is an emotion that seems to come out of nowhere. You have no reason to feel a strong emotion, but you do. This could be the Lord's emotion or the emotion of a person God wants you to pray for. You do not necessarily need to know whom you are praying for to be an effective intercessor.

Prayer burdens may come in the form of a verbal cue from the Lord or a faint impression in your spirit. You just know you need to pray. When you are carrying a prayer burden, you often have a strong sense of compassion—the Lord's compassion— for the object of your prayer. You are selfless in the moment, unconcerned about what other responsibilities are waiting. You are content to wait on the Lord.

Handling Prayer Burdens

When we are carrying prayer burdens, it is vital to stay in the Word of God so that the enemy does not overwhelm our soul. I like to pray Scripture as often as possible because the Word itself is an anchor for our soul and creates a clear division between the spirit and soul. Hebrews 4:12 (AMPC) reveals:

> For the Word that God speaks is alive and full of power [making it active, operative, energizing, and effective]; it is sharper than any two-edged sword, penetrating to the dividing line of the breath of life (soul) and [the immortal] spirit, and of joints and marrow [of the deepest parts of our nature], exposing *and* sifting *and* analyzing *and* judging the very thoughts and purposes of the heart.

In closing, I will leave you with another quote from E. M. Bounds from *Purpose in Prayer*:

> Desire burdens the chariot of prayer, and faith drives its wheels. Prayerless praying has no burden, because no sense of need; no ardency, because no vision, strength, or glow of faith. No mighty pressure to prayer, no holding on to God with the deathless, despairing grasp, "I will not let thee go except thou bless me." No utter self-abandon, lost in the throes of a desperate, pertinacious, and consuming plea: "Yet now if thou wilt forgive their sin—if not, blot me, I pray thee, out of thy book."[2]

Are you ready to pray?

Next-Level Prophetic Exercises

All prophets are intercessors, but not all intercessors are prophets. I have had "prophets" argue that point. My response: If you do not pray, you do not have anything to say. We can hear spontaneously from God anywhere at any time, but our prayer life fuels our prophetic. Here is how to cultivate a life of prayer that will allow you to step into the next level of your calling as prophet.

✓ Get this revelation deep inside you: Prayer is vital because prayer can unlock prophecy. Jeremiah 33:3 assures

105

us, "Call to Me, and I will answer you, and show you great and mighty things which you do not know."

✓ Prayer is your lifeline to God. Prophesying publicly without a strong prayer life could be the pitfall that pushes you into divination. Evaluate your prayer life.

✓ Are you prompt to respond to the Lord's prayer burdens? Do you roll over in bed when He is pulling on your spirit to pray or stand at attention waiting for prophetic directives? If you want God to trust you, rise up and pray when He calls.

✓ The prophet's mindset should be to watch and pray at all times. Do you have the mindset to "pray without ceasing" (1 Thessalonians 5:17)?

✓ Are you baptized in the Holy Spirit? Romans 8:26 tells us we do not know how to pray as we ought, but the Holy Spirit helps us. Apart from the Holy Spirit, we cannot operate at maximum effectiveness in prayer and prophecy, which go hand in hand.

In the next chapter, we explore the world of spiritual warfare as it relates to the prophetic. You will always have to battle demons to get to your next level.

8

Warfare: The Prophet's Mantra

Be well balanced (temperate, sober of mind), be
vigilant and cautious at all times; for that enemy of
yours, the devil, roams around like a lion roaring
[in fierce hunger], seeking someone to seize upon
and devour.

1 Peter 5:8 AMPC

There I was, barely sitting up while talking to a friend and trying to swallow semi-solid food after catching some violent virus
my daughter brought home from the mission field.

This was less than a week after discovering news so devastating I had no choice but to trade sleep for prayer just to
maintain. And that was only a week after someone in my inner
circle launched such a vicious verbal attack against me that I
wondered how I had misjudged his character so badly.

That was all just fourteen days of many where it seemed all
hell was breaking loose against me. Call it a season of spiritual
warfare. Call it a trial. Call it tribulation. Whatever you call it,
I was growing weary in well-doing and felt like I was about to

faint. And there, propped up on my couch, I was whining to my friend about the ongoing onslaught—whining and questioning, "Do you think everyone gets this much spiritual warfare, or am I doing something really wrong?"

Why So Much Spiritual Warfare?

I mean, most of my friends are dealing with the occasional common cold, cranky kid or flat tire. Meanwhile, I am laid out flat on my back with some strange illness while trying to process devastating news and enduring a Judas. Sometimes I wish I had my friends' problems instead of mine, but that is really not the right attitude, is it?

The Bible says:

> No temptation has overtaken you except such as is common to man; but God is faithful, who will not allow you to be tempted beyond what you are able, but with the temptation will also make the way of escape, that you may be able to bear it.
>
> 1 Corinthians 10:13 NKJV

The Bible also says, "Blessed is the man who endures temptation; for when he has been approved, he will receive the crown of life which the Lord has promised to those who love Him" (James 1:12 NKJV). Amen.

But that does not answer my question: Does everyone get this much spiritual warfare, or am I doing something wrong?

Furthermore, the Bible says:

> Beloved, do not think it strange concerning the fiery trial which is to try you, as though some strange thing happened to you; but rejoice to the extent that you partake of Christ's sufferings, that when His glory is revealed, you may also be glad with exceeding joy.
>
> 1 Peter 4:12–13 NKJV

Amen. I could go on and on with verses that tell us we will have tribulation but to take heart, with verses that tell us to be patient in tribulation, with verses that tell us we are blessed when others revile and persecute us and say all kinds of evil against us falsely because of Jesus. And I will say amen and amen. But that still does not answer my question: Does everyone get this much spiritual warfare, or am I doing something wrong?

A Supernatural Revelation

I would have my answer the morning after talking to my friend. That is when I met Rob Hoskins, president of OneHope, an international children's evangelism ministry. I was interviewing him for a cover story for *Charisma* magazine.[1] I had missed my first interview with him because I was plastered to my bed with the virus I mentioned. He was gracious enough to reschedule. Honestly, I had no idea the night before how I would make the thirty-minute drive and sit upright through the three-hour interview except for the grace of God. I was still that ill.

When I met Rob, I quickly discovered why Paul said it is not wise to compare ourselves with others (see 2 Corinthians 10:12). After serving me an espresso, Rob sat down at the conference room table, and within two minutes I had learned that he almost died the previous year from what the World Health Organization called the deadliest E. coli outbreak on record. Through that incident he discovered he had a fast-growing form of prostate cancer that could quickly move through the bladder wall and spread like wildfire through his body. Now that is spiritual warfare. He miraculously survived to tell the story with a smile.

When he got done telling that tale he shared his testimony of nearly going blind some years ago. Doctors told him they would try to save his eyes, but there was not much hope. His daughter was only a month old when he underwent pneumatic retinopexy, a surgery in which doctors inject a gas bubble inside the eye and then leave you lying facedown for weeks to heal. The father of lies invaded Rob's room in the night hours, and fear gripped his heart.

"God, if I can't see my daughter, if I can't see my wife, why did you put this vision and burden in me for the nations? Now I am going to be a blind man. I would just rather die. Just take me now," Hoskins said just before finally surrendering all to the Lord in complete consecration to His will—even if that meant blindness.

After his wife laid hands on him and started praying, the presence of Jesus filled the room, and Rob received three Scripture passages and a confirmation that he would be healed gradually. Now that is spiritual warfare. He was miraculously healed, and you can see the sparkle of joy in his eyes when he glorifies his Healer.

Learning to Trust God More

The point of the story was that the Lord wanted Rob to trust Him at greater levels. By trusting God through the attack of blindness—trusting Him for this gradual healing—Hoskins would be able to believe God for the miracles it would take to head a global ministry that aims to reach every child with God's Word by 2030. After experiencing that attack so long before, the E. coli and cancer were not so daunting.

Through faith and trust, God delivered Hoskins from blindness. God delivered him from E. coli. God delivered him from cancer. And I am sure God delivered him from other perils he did not have time to share with me.

As I sat there listening, all I could think of was how small my battles are compared to his. And that is not to say that I have not faced some intense spiritual battles, because I have.

(I am sure you have too.) At some level, it is all relative. That is why we cannot compare our spiritual warfare to another's spiritual warfare. It is just not wise to compare.

And so God gave me the answer to the question I was asking just twelve hours earlier: Do you think everyone gets this much spiritual warfare, or am I doing something really wrong? No, everyone does not get as much spiritual warfare as I do, or as you do. But some people get more—far more. And no, I am not doing anything wrong; I have not opened a door to the enemy. Quite the contrary, I am advancing the Kingdom of God, and I am a threat to the powers of darkness.

So are you, and you should remember that next time you take a hit for righteousness. Do not whine about the spiritual warfare. Rise above it. After all, you are seated in heavenly places in Christ Jesus. Do not fear the spiritual warfare. Trust God. Paul put it best when he said:

> Be anxious for nothing, but in everything by prayer and suppli-
> cation, with thanksgiving, let your requests be made known to
> God; and the peace of God, which surpasses all understanding,
> will guard your hearts and minds through Christ Jesus.
>
> Philippians 4:6–7 NKJV

Amen.

Prophets Bring Warfare

Prophets bring warfare. That is just a reality that you have to face in your ministry walk. There will be times—and probably many times—when you feel that all hell is breaking loose against you. Maybe you are under spiritual attack even as you read these words.

Well, I can relate. I recall another season when it felt like all hell broke loose against me. My mother underwent heart surgery, only to find out that the doctors could not fix the problem. According to the surgeon, she could throw a blood clot and have a massive stroke at any time. That kind of news tends to breed fear in your heart.

My then-fifteen-year-old daughter was left stranded in an international airport after a missions group failed to arrive on time to pick her up. Again, the spirit of fear launched a fiery dart. That same group neglected to collect the proper travel documents to give her entry into the foreign country to which they were traveling.

The next day a colleague I recommended for a preaching engagement failed to show up and attacked me when I suggested he needed to repent. I lost my rental car keys. I hit my head so hard I was too dizzy to drive. All the while I was living on virtually no sleep in a city seven hundred miles away from home, trying to seek God for the next chapter in my life.

Hand-to-Hand Combat

I could go on and on about the opposition I faced, but let's just say it felt like hell was breaking loose against me. I get it. Clearly the enemy did not want me to focus on consecrating myself during a time of prayer and fasting at the International House of Prayer in Atlanta. Clearly the enemy did not like the prophetic words I received there, which connected the dots to the next steps in my walk with God. Clearly the enemy was working to rob the seed the Holy Spirit had sown into my heart by stirring up a whirlwind of drama before, during and after I returned from Atlanta. It does not take a prophet to see all of this clearly. I was doing hand-to-hand combat with the enemy, fighting to receive and contain what the Lord was pouring into my spirit.

Maybe your story is not so dramatic. Maybe your story is much worse. Or maybe you are in a season of rest. But you are likely to feel like hell is breaking loose against you at some point in your life. And some people do seem to get a greater share of spiritual warfare than others.

So what do you do when you find yourself in the middle of hand-to-hand combat, when people you love are in danger even as others are stabbing you in the back? On a smaller scale, what do you do when you are just having a really bad day that you wish would end?

Hearing from God

The flesh, and maybe even the soul, wants to overreact. When the doctors said my mother's surgery was not successful and outlined the risks, I had to remain calm for the rest of the family. When my daughter used a stranger's cellphone to call me from an international airport saying the missions group was nowhere to be found, I had to keep my cool so I did not scare her.

When all hell breaks loose against you, the first challenge is not to overreact to what you are hearing in the natural. If you do, you will hinder your ability to hear from God—and you need to hear from God. If you quiet your soul, you are more likely to receive the direction you need to respond rather than react. Once you believe you have heard from God, take whatever action you can take in the natural and believe God that your obedience will yield a harvest.

Remember this: The devil is ultimately after your peace and your joy. Why do you think the Bible instructs us to rejoice in trials? James said to "count it all joy" when we encounter trials (James 1:2), and Peter told us not to think it is strange that a "fiery" trial has come our way—but to rejoice (1 Peter 4:12–13). So rejoice, and understand who the enemy is. It is not flesh and blood—and it is not God.

God did not cause my mother's heart problems. God did not cause the missions group to put my daughter in danger. God did not cause the preacher not to show up. But God permitted it. Likewise, God did not cause your woes. But nonetheless, you face trials and tribulations, and God is watching to see how you will respond. Will you keep your eyes on the Author and Finisher of your faith and remain in peace as a witness to the world, or will you freak out and melt down?

Consider Paul the apostle. He was a prisoner on a ship to Rome that was caught in a great storm. He was hungry from fasting. Nevertheless, he remained an encouragement to those around him—even to his captors. Paul continued to stand on God's Word—"I believe God that it will be just as it was told me" (Acts 27:25 NKJV). That is spiritual maturity.

When the ship wrecked, the soldiers planned to kill all the prisoners. Paul could have gotten in the flesh to defend himself. Instead, he continued to stand on God's Word. He kept believing God that it would be just as it was told him. And when a poisonous viper bit Paul, he did not have a panic attack. Instead, he continued to stand on God's Word. He kept believing God that it would be just as it was told him.

That must be our response when it feels like all hell is breaking loose against us. We have to go back to the Word—even if we have to get a concordance and look for verses that may relate to our specific trial—and find out what God has to say about the situation. Then we have to believe God that it will be just as it was told to us. And we seriously need to rejoice, because when all hell breaks loose against us, we can rest assured that all of heaven has our back. Only believe. Amen.

Discerning Demonic Strategies against Your Life

Lately I have been thinking about what I have been thinking about. In other words, I have been listening in more closely to the spiritual realm to discern the demonic activity trying to come against my mind and trying to come against people in my region.

When I was driving to church last week, for example, I suddenly heard thoughts like, *I'm so discouraged.* When I got in the car and started driving, I was happy as a lark, listening to classical music and praying. But when I crossed the line into Fort Lauderdale, thoughts of discouragement suddenly started bombarding my mind.

Although I have experienced this before, I almost fell for it. I started thinking about discouraging things going on in my life and in the world. By the time I pulled into the church parking lot, I was deflated. And then the Holy Spirit broke in and reminded me, "That's not your thought."

I called a friend and asked her if she was sensing discouragement in the spiritual climate, and she offered a confirmation. As a church we prayed against a spirit of discouragement, loneliness and oppression, and we felt something break. The joy of the Lord fell on the congregation, and we had a lovely service.

Of course, it is not always something in the city I am hearing. Sometimes the enemy is targeting my mind with destructive or seductive thoughts. Yes, Satan does put thoughts in our minds. Consider Luke 4:3, where "the devil said" things to Jesus. The devil is a spirit, a fallen angel, who moves in the spirit realm. He does not need a body to talk to you any more than God needs a body to talk to you. Just as the devil talked to Jesus, he is still talking to people today.

Lately I have been thinking about what I have been thinking about. In other words, I have been keener on discerning the thoughts that are floating around in my mind and their origin. Did you know that you could go throughout much of your day on autopilot? You can get dressed for work in the morning, drive to the office, drive home, cook dinner and watch television at night while your mind is reasoning through all sorts of thoughts.

We need to start paying attention to what we are thinking about and the origin of those thoughts. We need to be quicker to listen to the inner talk going on in our souls. When we do, we will start to discern the demonic strategies against our lives. For example, you may hear thoughts like, *No one appreciates me.* If you reason that thought out in your mind, you will end up a little angry, maybe resentful and eventually bitter. That thought will eventually drive your behavior toward the people you feel underappreciate you.

God's Thoughts versus Satan's Thoughts

Where are your thoughts coming from? God's thoughts are "higher than" our thoughts (Isaiah 55:9). Satan's thoughts are lower than God's thoughts. Which way our internal thought life sways depends in part on our reasoning. God's thoughts toward us are "of peace and not of evil, to give [us] a future and a hope (Jeremiah 29:11 NKJV). Satan's thoughts toward us are of war and not of goodness, to give us a future without hope. Which way our internal thought life leans depends in part on our reasoning.

Although our thoughts will never reach the height of God's thoughts—the Creator is all-knowing—our thoughts need not reach the lows of Satan's thoughts. In other words, God gave us the ability to reason and a free will to choose what we think about—whether thoughts of peace and hope or thoughts of evil and hopelessness. So stop and think about what you are thinking about.

And know this: Many of the negative words we speak and the ungodly actions we take originate from the seed of a thought Satan whispers to our souls. That seed can grow into demon-inspired weeds as our minds reason out the thought. That seed can spark a fire in our souls, so to speak, that fuels more wrong thoughts, wrong words and wrong deeds.

When the enemy plants a vain imagination in our minds, we have two choices: cast it down or meditate on it. When we meditate on vain imaginations, we tend to connect demonic dots that create skewed pictures of reality. Believing what we see in our thought life is real, we talk ourselves into taking action based on a wrong perception. That action could be a negative attitude toward people, an angry outburst that hurts someone you love or a sinful behavior that leads you into bondage. But believe this: It all starts with a thought.

There is a war in your mind, whether you discern it or not. I urge you to start discerning what is going on in your mind, will and emotions, and then to bring your mind into submission to the mind, will and emotions of God by His grace. Paul put it this way:

> For though we walk in the flesh, we do not war according to the flesh. For the weapons of our warfare are not carnal but mighty in God for pulling down strongholds, casting down arguments and every high thing that exalts itself against the knowledge of God, bringing every thought into captivity to the obedience of Christ, and being ready to punish all disobedience when your obedience is fulfilled.
>
> 2 Corinthians 10:3–6 NKJV

Amen.

Discerning Demonic Hindrances

I will admit it. There have been times when I thought the devil was in my way, and it was really the Holy Spirit preventing me. There were other times when I thought the Holy Spirit was opening the door and it was really the devil tapping into the idolatry in my own heart to set me up for a mess.

I have grown up quite a lot in Christ since then, but we are all prone to miss it from time to time. Understanding how the Holy Spirit leads and how the devil deceives can help you follow the steps the Lord has ordered for you instead of falling into the roaring lion's trap.

We can take a lesson from the apostle Paul, who keenly observed the difference between his own plans, the Holy Spirit's plans and the devil's plans. Paul was called to preach the Gospel to the Gentiles, and he got about the Father's business with as much zeal as he formerly displayed in persecuting the church. Paul traveled the world over in his day, but when he and his apostolic team went through certain cities to preach the Word, the Holy Spirit stopped him in favor of a more strategic mission. In Acts 16:6–10 (NKJV) Luke records:

> Now when they had gone through Phrygia and the region of Galatia, they were forbidden by the Holy Spirit to preach the word in Asia. After they had come to Mysia, they tried to go into Bithynia, but the Spirit did not permit them. So passing by Mysia, they came down to Troas. And a vision appeared to Paul in the night. A man of Macedonia stood and pleaded with him, saying, "Come over to Macedonia and help us." Now after he had seen the vision, immediately we sought to go to Macedonia, concluding that the Lord had called us to preach the gospel to them.

Paul concluded that the Lord wanted him to preach the Gospel in Macedonia only after the Holy Spirit twice prevented him from preaching in other cities, then gave him a vision that clearly laid out the next leg of his missionary journey. In other words, Paul had his plans, but the Holy Spirit had a different plan. Paul could have mistakenly blamed the devil for the obstacles to getting the Gospel out in Phyrgia and the region of Galatia and Bithynia, but he discerned it was the Holy Spirit—not the devil—preventing him from fulfilling his mission.

The story was altogether different in Paul's endeavors to visit the church at Thessalonica. Paul writes, "Therefore we wanted to come to you—even I, Paul, time and again—but Satan hindered us" (1 Thessalonians 2:18 NKJV). We do not know exactly how Paul determined it was Satan hindering him rather than the Holy Spirit preventing him or what Satan may have done to hinder him. But Paul was certain the devil was to blame.

Discerning Satanic Hindrances

Sometimes it is obvious that the Holy Spirit is preventing you or that the devil is thwarting you. But sometimes it is not so obvious. So how do you tell the difference?

1. Ask the Holy Spirit what is going on.

First of all we need to pray and ask the Lord what is going on. When in doubt, our best first move is to trust in the Lord and not on our own understanding. Just because we have seen a pattern in how the Holy Ghost moves or how Satan works does not mean we can automatically presume who is behind something. That said, there are some discernable demonic hints.

2. Did God already tell you to do it?

If you are convinced that the Holy Spirit expressly told you to do something and you are meeting with obstacles, it is likely the enemy trying to prevent fruit for the Kingdom. Satan constantly works to hinder God's plan, even though he is already defeated.

3. What is the objective of the hindrance?

Any hindrance that keeps you from getting closer to God is not from God. Satan will set up idols in our lives hoping we will go after the promotion, the money, the entertainment, the fame or something else. Of course, he uses our own flesh and soulish desires to distract us. You cannot really blame the devil.

4. What's going through your mind?

The Word says we should think on good things. If the hindrance you face is coming in the form of unpleasant thoughts and fearful imaginations, that is not God speaking to you. That is the devil's way of getting you into fear, doubt and unbelief.

Remember, we are not wrestling against flesh and blood— but we are wrestling. The key is to wrestle with the enemy and not with God. In other words, we do not want to be resisting God when we should be resisting the enemy, and we do not want to be cooperating with the enemy when we should be cooperating with God. The enemy is walking around like a roaring lion seeking someone to devour. God's eyes roam to and fro over the earth in order "to strengthen those whose hearts are fully committed to him" (2 Chronicles 16:9 NIV).

The bottom line is, do what Paul did: "Commit your way to the LORD, trust also in Him, and He shall bring it to pass" (Psalm 37:5 NKJV). No devil in hell can keep you from God's will if you are sold out to His plan.

Never Let the Devil See You Sweat

Never let the devil see you sweat. If your best friend betrays you, do not put your disappointment on display. If you cannot pay your mortgage, do not verbally doom your financial fate. If the doctor gives you a bad report, do not speak death over your life. If you just feel like giving up, do not voice your resignation.

There is no faith in circumstantial fretting. Our frustration and fear is what causes us to overheat and sometimes boil over. Why not decide by your will to agree with the Word of God and receive the grace you need to overcome the disappointment, financial stress, health issues and despair? Why not walk in Philippians 1:28? Pick whatever translation inspires you. Here are a couple of choices. The Amplified Bible, Classic Edition (AMPC) reads:

> And do not [for a moment] be frightened or intimidated in anything by your opponents and adversaries, for such [constancy and fearlessness] will be a clear sign (proof and seal) to them of [their impending] destruction, but [a sure token and evidence] of your deliverance and salvation, and that from God.

If you prefer more modern language, try the Contemporary English Version (CEV): "Be brave when you face your enemies. Your courage will show them that they are going to be destroyed, and it will show you that you will be saved. God will make all of this happen, and he has blessed you" (verses 28–29).

Beloved, we need to be doers of this Word! I have read this verse over and over and over (and over and over and over) again, but one day when I opened my Bible I saw something I had never seen before. It is glaringly obvious at some level, but bear with me, because maybe the Holy Ghost will help you connect the dots like He just did for me.

Here is the point: Walking in Philippians 1:28 is spiritual warfare waged from our position in Christ. Think about it for a minute. Was Christ ever for a moment frightened or intimidated by His opponents and adversaries? No, He was not. In fact, Christ's constancy and fearlessness were clear signs, proof and a seal that God was with Him. He was not "anxious about anything, but in every situation, by prayer and petition, with thanksgiving," He presented His "requests to God. And the peace of God, which transcends all understanding," guarded His heart and mind (Philippians 4:6–7 NIV). We have that same promise from our position in Christ. And that is where we war from.

That peace belongs to us. That stability belongs to us. That faith belongs to us. When we let the devil see us sweat, so to speak, we are demonstrating that we have more fear of the devil than fear of the Lord. When we start talking about all of our problems and walking in worry, we are demonstrating that we have more faith in what the devil is showing us than faith in what the Lord has told us. When we let the devil see us sweat, we are not in complete unity with God because we are not doing what His Word says. We may believe it is true, but faith without action is dead.

Who Is Going to Get the Glory?

When you run into a trial, who gets your attention? Jesus or the devil? God deserves all the glory all the time—and He gets glory when you do His Word because then you get what He promised.

God tells us over and again not to fear. And we know that "God has not given us a spirit of fear, but of power and of love and of a sound mind (2 Timothy 1:7 NKJV). God has given us Holy Ghost power "over all the power of the enemy" (Luke 10:19). He has given us His "perfect love," which casts out all fear when we embrace it (1 John 4:18). And He has given us a sound mind and a discerning spirit so we will not fall into the snare of the enemy.

So how do we manage not to let the devil see us sweat—not to visibly and verbally react to the circumstances around us—when the storms are raging? How do we trust God for the totality of His salvation, which includes deliverance, safety, healing and health? The answer is simple: Look at everything from God's perspective.

Next question: How can you find God's perspective? Well, His Word is His perspective. God does not break a sweat when your daughter rebels. He does not start biting His nails when you lose your job. He does not have a nervous breakdown when you get a bad report from the doctor. No, God laughs at the enemy because He knows the end of your story (see Psalm 2:4).

How do you keep God's perspective? Think about what is true, noble, just, pure, lovely and of a good report (see Philippians 4:8). There are plenty of promises—more than seven thousand, actually—to meditate on that will build your faith and send fear running seven different ways. There is no way to get knots in your stomach when you meditate on God's virtue and praiseworthiness. There is only peace and victory.

And remember, everything on this earth is temporal. "No weapon that is formed against you" can prosper (Isaiah 54:17). Not really. The devil is waiting for the satisfaction of a single bead of perspiration to drop from your brow—or a single word of doubt to cross your lips. But God is also watching, and He has equipped you to stand against the wiles of the devil as you await the assured promise of His deliverance. So keep your eyes on eternity and never let the devil see you sweat. Give God the glory for your deliverance. He is faithful.

Standing in the Gap for a Nation

Ezekiel was a patriotic prophet. He proved his love for the nation of Israel over and again in ways that were sacrificial, uncomfortable and downright humbling. In fact, in order to demonstrate the heart and mind of God, Ezekiel executed some of the strangest prophetic acts in the Bible. In total submission to the Spirit of God, Ezekiel lay on one side of his body for months on end, then the other.

Ezekiel was not the only patriotic prophet in the Word of God though. There are many nationalistic *nabis* in the Word of God. Indeed, prophets who were loyal to God and country at all costs mark the annals of the prophetic ministry. I pray that this same spirit will sweep over every prophet in every nation today.

Whether you are a watchman assigned to the United States of America, the United Kingdom, New Zealand, or some other nation that is under attack from dominion-seeking false religions, oppressive governments or secular humanistic ideology (and it is hard to think of a nation where that description does not apply), your role is to stand in the gap and intercede for

God's will. The way I see it, instead of boasting about how we are "prophets to the nations" we should make doubly sure that we are prophets to our own nations first. After all, they say, charity begins at home.

In 2007 the Lord gave me a powerful prophetic word for the United States—and a spiritual warfare strategy that is so simple a child could implement it. But that revelation did not fall into my lap while I was crying out to God for a new car and financial increase. No, it came after days of repeatedly standing in the gap for this nation and its leaders, pleading with Him for mercy, petitioning for a hedge of protection and repenting for the sin that is committed in this land.

Instead of pronouncing angry judgment on some states and declaring curses over others, as we so often see in today's prophetic circles, I broke the curses and bound the enemy's plan to kill, steal and destroy. I know many of you are doing the same thing, and I thank God for your faithfulness. Yes, God's discipline is upon our nation, but prophets should not proclaim it with joy; they should share it with weeping.

Falling on your face in deep repentance and asking God to heal the land may not sound as exciting as hollering at the devil and fervently flailing your arms. And I agree that it is not as much fun in practice, but it is not about showing off spiritual warfare skills, is it? It is about standing in the office of the prophet, functioning in that role the way God directs. There are times to shout the victory the way the Israelites did at Jericho. And there are times to weep and cry in repentance, as did Jeremiah. I would urge you, prophets and intercessors, to seek God for the prophetic warfare strategy that God wants to execute in this time and this season.

Remember King David, a prophet and a mighty man of war? David consulted God with this memorable query: "Shall I go up?" (see 2 Samuel 2:1 NKJV; 2 Samuel 5:19; 1 Chronicles 14:10). But as David matured, he was not always satisfied with a yes or no answer from his Commander in chief. He depended on the

Lord to offer him an assurance of victory, a specific, customized prophetic warfare strategy and specific instructions for battle.

Like David, our spiritual warfare must be waged from a position of victory. That means knowing who you are in Christ and "the exceeding greatness of His power toward us who believe" (Ephesians 1:19 NKJV).

Pressing in for prophetic strategies is a sign of maturity because, I daresay, young prophets may spend a lot of time screaming at the devil, or as the apostle Paul put it, buffeting the air (see 1 Corinthians 9:26). In doing so, it is quite possible that they could wind up fighting against the very will of God.

Know this: Although God's battle plans are always successful, they may differ from skirmish to skirmish. That is why we need prophetic strategies. Just because Joshua and the Israelites marched around Jericho seven times, let out a shout and watched the walls fall down does not mean that is applicable for every situation (see Joshua 6). Likewise, just because Jehoshaphat and his crew defeated the enemy with praise and thanksgiving without ever lifting a finger to fight does not mean that will work in all occasions (see 2 Chronicles 20). Praise is always appropriate, but sometimes you have to enter into the battle with the whole armor of God and fight.

David understood this. When he encountered the Philistines at the Valley of Rephaim the first time, he "inquired of the LORD, 'Shall I go and attack the Philistines? Will you deliver them into my hands?' The LORD answered him, 'Go, for I will surely deliver the Philistines into your hands'" (2 Samuel 5:19 NIV). David was victorious in battle, but he did not let it go to his head. When the Philistines came up and spread out in the valley the second time, David did not make presumptions. He inquired of the Lord again. This time, the Lord had a different battle plan:

> Do not go straight up, but circle around behind them and attack them in front of the poplar trees. As soon as you hear the

sound of marching in the tops of the poplar trees, move quickly, because that will mean the Lord has gone out in front of you to strike the Philistine army.

2 Samuel 5:23–24 NIV

Of course, David and his mighty men won again, striking down the Philistines all the way from Gibeon to Gezer.

It is important to note here that David was fighting for his nation. His acts were patriotic. He was a deliverer. He was a warrior. He was a reformer—all earmarks of true prophets. Sure, David could have rested in his popularity after defeating Goliath. He could have sent his army out to do the fighting. Or he could have rushed out in arrogance against any and every enemy, whether it was God's timing or not. But David did not do that. His concern was not merely for himself. It was for the nation of Israel.

David's battle plans often started with prayer: "Shall I go up?" He sought prophetic warfare strategies that preserved a nation from its enemies by putting God's will first. I challenge you, prophets and intercessors, to follow David's example. Stand for your nation. Seek prophetic strategies. And watch God restore Kingdom culture on earth just as it is in heaven.

When You Feel Like You Are Fighting Alone

I am in a war, and so are you. If you feel like you are fighting alone, take heart. You are not the only one who has ever felt this way. And you are not really alone. No, not really.

I walk through seasons when it seems like I am outnumbered by principalities and powers, even though I know God and I make a majority. I know if God is for me it does not really matter who is against me, but I feel like I am on the battlefield all by myself. I know there is no temptation that is not common to man, but I feel like no one really understands what I am going through. This is a common feeling among prophets and prophetic people.

Indeed, prophets can face such extreme spiritual warfare that they are sure they are the only ones in the world who are standing for God's will—and taking the demonic heat for it. I call this the Elijah Syndrome.

Two times Elijah told the Lord he was the only one of the prophets left and people were out to get him. He pointed out how he was outnumbered by the 450 Baal prophets (1 Kings 18:22) and how there was a price on his head (1 Kings 19:10, 14).

Elijah was not the only prophet in the Bible who felt he was fighting an uphill battle without reinforcements. Surely, Jeremiah, Isaiah and others felt the pain of loneliness on and off the theater of spiritual war. I imagine people told them, "I'm praying for you, Jerry," but went fishing or enjoyed the Sabbath instead.

Indeed, for all the well-intentioned Christians who tell you they are standing with you and praying for you, far fewer actually follow up on the intercessory initiative. After all, they are also in a war. And they have stuff flying at them too.

Battling Loneliness in the Midst of War

The prophet's walk can be a lonely one, but in the midst of the spiritual warfare the intensity of the witchcraft and imaginations can make you feel especially isolated, rejected and abandoned by those you think should be taking up arms on your behalf.

Understand this: Loneliness is one of the weapons of the enemy's warfare against your mind, intended to pressure you to lay down your weapons and stop fighting. The reality is that it is unlikely you are fighting alone, but even if you are, the Lord is with you.

The prophet David clearly felt alone when he wrote, "When my father and my mother forsake me, then the LORD will take care of me" (Psalm 27:10 NKJV). The Lord encouraged the prophet Moses with these words: "Be strong and of good courage, do not fear nor be afraid of them; for the LORD your God, He is the One who goes with you. He will not leave you nor forsake you" (Deuteronomy 31:6 NKJV).

Prophet, do not fall into the Elijah Syndrome—or if you have already, allow God to set you straight the way He did the lonely spiritual warrior: "I have reserved seven thousand in Israel, all whose knees have not bowed to Baal, and every mouth that has not kissed him" (1 Kings 19:18 NKJV).

Over the years, I have learned there are certain battles I do have to fight alone—but I am not really alone. God is with me. He is my refuge, my strength and a very present help in time of need (see Psalm 46:1). He will move on the hearts of intercessors I have never met to support me in the battle and, if He has to, He will send angels to battle principalities in the heavens to get me the answers I need, just like He did for the prophet Daniel.

The Lord Is a Warrior

David's mighty men were indeed fighting alone from a natural perspective, but it is clear that the Lord's anointing was upon them. Make no mistake, the battle is the Lord's (see 1 Samuel 17:47). But He often uses us as His warriors in the natural realm, as a "battle-ax" (Jeremiah 51:20). When you go to battle in faith for His purposes, the anointing will meet you, and you will overcome, even if you have to fight alone.

The Bible makes it clear in Eleazar's case that "the LORD brought about a great victory that day" (2 Samuel 23:10) and again in Shammah's case that "the LORD brought about a great victory" (verse 12). These men were indeed fighting alone, but they did not curl up into a fetal position and whine about it. They stepped out into God's will as battle-axes, and the Lord anointed them to do mighty exploits for His glory. He can do the same for you.

As for Paul, at his first defense, when no one stood with him, note the preface to his statement and the conclusion. Maybe you can relate.

> Demas has forsaken me, having loved this present world, and has departed for Thessalonica—Crescens for Galatia, Titus for Dalmatia. . . . Alexander the coppersmith did me much harm.
>
> 2 Timothy 4:10, 14 NKJV

Paul truly did fight alone at times. But listen to Paul's response to all this spiritual warfare and set your mind to take the same approach when you meet with betrayal, abandonment, false accusations and persecution—or any other warfare—for the sake of Christ:

> But the Lord stood with me and strengthened me, so that the message might be preached fully through me, and that all the Gentiles might hear. Also I was delivered out of the mouth of the lion. And the Lord will deliver me from every evil work and preserve me for His heavenly kingdom. To Him be glory forever and ever. Amen!
>
> verses 17–18 NKJV

Some days it may feel like you are fighting alone. From a natural perspective, you may be. But the Lord is faithful. This battle is ultimately the Lord's, and when you stand for Him—and when all hell breaks loose against you for that stance—He will strengthen you. He will anoint you. He will deliver you. He will preserve you. Amen!

Next-Level Prophetic Exercises

The enemy hates the voice of God and will fight the release of truth at every turn. If you carry a prophetic mantle, you also need to embrace a warfare mantle. The spiritual battles will be fierce, but if you fight, you will win. Do not let the warfare bring fear. Rise up and know that Christ has already won the victory—but that you have to enforce it.

✓ Beware the "no warfare" heresy circulating in some prophetic ministry camps. The Bible speaks of our need to fight over and over again. There is no cease-fire in the spirit. You cannot lay your weapons down and expect the enemy not to attack. Worshiping the Lord is one way to defeat the enemy, as we see in Scripture, but it is not the only defense against the devil.

✓ You cannot change the reality that prophets bring warfare, so accept it now. By accepting warfare, you are not inviting warfare; you are preparing for victory.

✓ Meditate on who you are in Christ and your authority in Him. This will give you faith that makes you fierce in the Spirit.

✓ Ask the Holy Spirit for a stronger gift of discernment so you can rightly discern the enemy's approach and can combat him before he releases the first punch.

In the next chapter, we will examine the call for holiness as it relates to getting to the next level in your prophetic gifting.

9

Holiness: The Prophet's Cry

When I was first born again, God took me to the back side of nowhere—my wilderness place—to remove me from the evil influences of my past. He took me to a small country town where I did not know anyone and no one knew me so He could set me apart for Himself.

Of course, evil is everywhere you go, and it soon found me. Slowly but surely I made new friends, and those new friends were not exactly holy. Oh, do not get me wrong. They went to church religiously and called Jesus Lord, but their lifestyles did not match their Sunday confession.

One evening these new friends came over with a six-pack of beer. I was newly born again—I had been saved about three months—and my mind was not renewed to the perils of alcohol. So when my newfound friends handed me a can of beer, I cracked it open and settled in to watch the movie. I did not even drink beer before I was saved, but because I was all alone in a new place, I decided to go with the flow. I did not realize how unholy that flow was.

After a few sips I found myself on my bedroom floor doubled over in pain. It was agonizing. I was not sure what to make of it. I ate some antacids, and that did not help—because these violent cramps I was experiencing were not coming from a natural source. I had grieved the Holy Spirit, and I believe He was delivering me from something.

As I lay in a ball on the floor, the Holy Spirit began to speak with me about choices and how they would ripple through my life and the lives of others. After that, I set my heart not to allow things in my house that offended God. My stance on sin under my roof cost me some friends, but I would rather be an enemy of the world and a friend to God than the other way around (see James 4:4).

From that point on I started striving for holiness. I did not really even understand some of the biblical concepts the Holy Spirit was teaching me, but I pressed in to purity. I stopped watching television, except TV preachers. I only listened to Christian music. I fell asleep reading the Bible at night with the light on.

I was not perfect, and I am still not. Thankfully, God does not expect us to be perfect. He just wants us to press toward the mark of maturity. He wants us to be quick to repent and seek His mercy, grace, forgiveness and strength to overcome our flesh. Many years after that painful encounter with the Holy Spirit, I am still pressing in to intimacy with Him that will change me from glory to glory.

Intimacy with the Devil

There is a lot of talk about intimacy with God in the Body of Christ, and I believe we should continue emphasizing His invitation into deeper relationship with Him. But for all the talk of how intimacy with God leads to spiritual pregnancies that ultimately lead to birthing God's will, there is a flip side. You cannot be intimate with the devil and not get pregnant with sin. And if you get pregnant with sin and carry sin to term, you will birth corruption.

> Be not deceived. God is not mocked. For whatever a man sows, that will he also reap. For the one who sows to his own flesh will from the flesh reap corruption, but the one who sows to the Spirit will from the Spirit reap eternal life.
>
> Galatians 6:7–8

Do not deceive yourself. You cannot lie down with the devil and stand and resist the devil at the same time. Another translation of that Scripture reads: "For he who sows to his own flesh (lower nature, sensuality) will from the flesh reap decay and ruin and destruction, but he who sows to the Spirit will from the Spirit reap eternal life" (verse 8 AMPC).

Do not deceive yourself. You cannot pursue holiness and sin at the same time. You cannot submit to the Most High God and your lower nature at the same time. But you can choose to identify with the reality that you have been united with Christ in the likeness of His death and resurrection. You can meditate on the fact that you have been crucified with Him and are no longer a slave to sin; you are a slave to righteousness (see Romans 6:18).

> Likewise, you also consider yourselves to be dead to sin, but alive to God through Jesus Christ our Lord. Therefore do not let sin reign in your mortal body, that you should obey it in its lusts. Do not yield your members to sin as instruments of unrighteousness, but yield yourselves to God, as those who are alive from the dead, and your bodies to God as instruments of righteousness. For sin shall not have dominion over you, for you are not under the law, but under grace.
>
> Romans 6:11–14

No one who abides in Jesus practices sin (see 1 John 3:6). That does not mean Christians—or even prophets—do not sin. There is a difference between sinning and practicing sin, or being intimate with the devil. The one who sins and is quick to repent is growing in grace. The one who is practicing sin is taking "the grace of God in vain" (2 Corinthians 6:1) and frustrating the grace of God (see Galatians 2:21).

Hear me. Sin will dull your prophetic edge faster than anything else and prevent you from cutting through to the next level. Holiness, by contrast, will sharpen your prophetic edge. If we want to hear more clearly from the Lord, we need to work with the Holy Spirit to "cleanse ourselves from all filthiness of the flesh and spirit, perfecting holiness in the fear of God" (2 Corinthians 7:1). If we want to see more clearly in the Spirit, we need to pursue "holiness without which no one will see the Lord" (Hebrews 12:14).

You Cannot Make Yourself Holy

I suppose I am getting ahead of myself. What does it mean to be holy? I am not talking about being religious, mind you. I am talking about what God has in mind when His Word says things like this:

> For I am the LORD your God. You shall therefore sanctify yourselves, and you shall be holy, for I am holy. Neither shall you defile yourselves with any manner of crawling thing that moves on the ground.
>
> Leviticus 11:44

God "has not called us to impurity," but to holiness (1 Thessalonians 4:7 AMPC). If we cleanse ourselves from what is dishonorable, we can be vessels for honorable use, set apart as holy and useful to God for good works (see 2 Timothy 2:21).

But, again, what does God expect from His prophets and prophetic people? *Bible Study Tools*'s King James Version New

Testament Greek Lexicon clarifies that the Hebrew word for "holy" in Leviticus 11:14 is *qadowsh*, which means "sacred, holy, Holy One, saint and set apart." The Greek word for "holiness" in 1 Thessalonians 4:7 comes from *hagiasmos*, which means "consecration, purification, the effect of consecration, and the sanctification of heart and life." Although moral purity is part of it, what God is trying to drive home is our decision to dedicate ourselves to Him, belonging to Him. It is a relational concept that leads to moral behavior rather than a set of rules and regulations that produces moral behavior.

Holiness is complete devotion to the work of God. That means we have to purify ourselves and sanctify ourselves constantly for His use, because the spirit of the world is ever working to distract us from His love. If we are going to see His visions, then we should guard our eye gates. If we are going to hear His words, then we should guard our ear gates. If we are going to speak His words, then we should watch our mouths. We need to be devoted to the Word of God because we cannot prophesy beyond our knowledge of God's Word.

Old Testament prophets were models of holiness, study and closeness to God. Think about it for a minute. Would Isaiah have watched some of the junk coming out of Hollywood? Would Elijah have listened to some of the lustful lyrics they play on the radio today?

You may say, well, things are different today. But God is not different. We have to die to our own selfish desires and make His desires our desires. We have to crave intimacy with God. That is true holiness. That said, we cannot make ourselves holy. The late David Wilkerson drove that point home in a 1982 sermon called "Be Ye Holy." He said:

> Church history is filled with ridiculous ideas on how to be holy. I have read of monks who slept on bundles of thorns and piles of broken glass. Others bound one foot, hopping around on

one foot until they lost the use of the other. [Simeon] Stylites stood for thirty years on top of a column, and when too weak to stay there, he had a post erected and chained himself to it. In the Middle Ages, long processions of flagellants traveled from country to country, moaning, weeping, singing sad songs of repentance, and whipping their bare backs as they marched. Thousands joined these processions in an effort to "whip out the evil."[1]

No, we cannot make ourselves holy by outward rules and regulations and religious exercises. But we can choose to exchange the sexually charged television shows for Bible study times. We can choose to trade violent movies for worship services. We can choose to spend less time on social media and more time in prayer. We can, by our will, "seek first the kingdom of God and His righteousness" (Matthew 6:33) and put our faith in the One who promised to complete the "good work" He started in us to perfect us in holiness (Philippians 1:6).

Charles Spurgeon, remembered as the prince of preachers in the nineteenth century, put it this way: "A faith which works not for purification will work for putrefaction. Unless our faith makes us pine after holiness . . . it is no better than the faith of devils, and perhaps it is not even so good as that. . . . A holy man is the workmanship of the Holy Spirit."[2] Elsewhere he elaborated, "I believe the holier a man becomes the more he mourns over the unholiness which remains in him."[3]

Do not receive the enemy's condemning thoughts if you are falling short of this mark. We "grow in the grace" of holiness (2 Peter 3:18). One cannot expect a new believer to attain to the measure of holiness and repentance of another who has been walking with the Lord for decades. We are sanctified, but we are also being sanctified. But, as Spurgeon wrote, "You are a stranger to holiness if your heart does not feel that it revolts at the thought of sin."[4]

Dealing with Demons from Your Past

Do not look back—unless you need to deal with demons from your past that continue to pull you out of God's will and into sin.

Some of us have dramatic testimonies of how God delivered us from dark places into which even your typical sinner does not venture. But if we are not truly free from the demonic influences that held us in bondage, we could fall back into the snare of the enemy once again. We are forgiven from our past sins, but sometimes we must deal with our past demons.

I am a big advocate of not looking back. Unless I am sharing my testimony to help another, I do not talk much about the past. After all, I am a new creature in Christ. The old Jennifer has passed away. I was crucified with Christ, and I am no longer living for myself. I am letting Christ live His life through me. My position in Christ is clearly spelled out in the Word of God, but that does not mean when I got saved I was immediately delivered from demons of the past that plagued my soul. I am not talking about character flaws or immaturity. I am talking about demonic strongholds like drug use that, left unchecked, would have ultimately destroyed me.

If we do not deal with the demons from our past, the devil will come at a more opportune time and try to steal, kill and destroy us. I am not suggesting here that a relatively stable and growing Christian embark on a guided expedition in their soul to dig up something that is not really there and magnify it, or visit a deliverance minister just in case there is a demon that needs to be cast out. Doing those things can cause problems that did not exist. Indeed, many issues are just our emotions raging, and we need to learn to submit our feelings to the Word and renew our mind.

Demons from the past are often recognizable as persistent issues that hold you back from God's best. When you encounter one, it is like hitting a wall that you cannot leap over, get around, dig under or break through. It is a bondage. Often deliverance ministry is required. But even then, you have to do your part.

You have probably heard the phrase "his past came back to haunt him" or talk of a "ghost from the past." I am not talking here about past sins people committed, renounced and repented of. That is under the blood. I am talking about deep emotional wounds that were buried alive and did not make it to the cross. Oftentimes, a demon will attach itself to those old wounds and manifest through issues like fear, addiction, anger or depression. There could also be generational curses at work. What happened in our past is not always our fault. Others can inflict deep wounds on us without any causative action on our part. Perhaps we were not equipped to deal with the fallout, so we built up protective walls or destructive habits that sabotage our relationships, our jobs, our homes and our very lives.

You have no doubt read the news headlines of prominent ministers whose past came back to haunt them. Some were sexually molested as children and later fell into homosexual affairs as adults. Others were addicted to drugs and alcohol, and the pressure of ministry caused them to return to those spirits for comfort and escape, only to sober up to spirits like guilt and condemnation.

But let's drill down beyond the headlines into the everyday lives of believers. Let's bring this home. Dealing with demons from the past does not always mean dealing with sexual immorality or drug abuse. Demons from the past can simply mean resolving unforgiveness toward someone who hurt you or seeking forgiveness from one you have hurt so you can rid yourself of the guilt that torments your mind.

I believe the Holy Spirit is faithful to bring to our attention the issues that we need to deal with, if we do not already see them. He may do that one-on-one or use a trusted person in your life to point out a problem in love. When we can see a demonic stronghold, whether subtly in our thoughts or fully manifest through our actions, we need to get help. If we are well aware that demons from our past are leading us into dangerous temptations, and especially if we are falling into the trap, we need to get help. We need to deal with the demons of our past.

So how do you do that? Acknowledge that there is a problem. Confront it courageously. Stop running from it. Do not deny it is there. Do not try to build your walls higher. Take off the mask you have been using to disguise the pain you are going through. That requires humility, but humility opens the door to God's grace. Get some help from trusted Christians in your life who are equipped to help you find the deliverance and healing you need in Christ. Do not worry about what other people are going to think if they know the truth. If they are discerning people, they probably already know you are struggling. Where you find yourself may not be your fault, but getting free requires you to take responsibility for your choices now.

The same old emotions may continue to come even after you deal with the demons of your past. But when Jesus sets you free by the power of the Holy Ghost, you are free indeed. Once you confront these demons, you will gain a new perspective. When those old emotions, those old thoughts and temptations, come rolling back around, you will be able to recognize what is happening and respond rather than react to the demon's taunt. As you continue to do this, you will build your spiritual muscles, and eventually the demon will give up and go bother someone else. God will meet you at the point of your decision and help you overcome the demons of your past. Victory belongs to you. Decide to walk in it.

Breaking the Power of Vicious Circles and Demonic Cycles

Have you ever felt like you keep repeating the same bad day? You stay spiritually disciplined to break through the demonic attacks, but the harder you try the greater the backlash?

Look at your warfare good and hard. Is there a pattern to the madness? Is it seasonal? Does the warfare rise up when you enter certain types of ministry or when you get around certain people?

Before we go on, let me state emphatically that not every obstacle or setback we face in life is rooted in demonic activity. Becoming super skilled in spiritual warfare is not going to solve all of your problems, because all of your problems are not originating with demons. Getting hyperfocused on identifying demons and tearing down strongholds can actually perpetuate the vicious cycle. What we magnify tends to manifest. Magnify the devil, and he seems bigger in your eyes. Magnify Jesus, and His glory inspires you to overcome by His grace.

With all that said, there are demonic cycles that make your head spin and seem to make no sense whatsoever—except they do. Demonic powers work to gain toeholds, footholds and strongholds in our minds that skew our perspective so that we are blinded to the trap that lies just ahead. A demonic cycle is not just a character flaw or a bad habit. It is deeper than that. It is rooted in a lie that you believe, except you do not know it is a lie. The nature of deception is an unawareness that you are deceived.

Demonic cycles can be somewhat like generational curses but usually are reserved for the individual who took the bait. I walked through a demonic cycle of sickness for three years before I took a stand against it. I had accepted that every November through March I would get the flu, bronchitis and have bad allergies. Demonic cycles can also lead you to job hop, church hop, relationship hop or various instabilities.

Before I knew the Lord, I walked in a demonic cycle called self-sabotage. I had an all-or-nothing personality. In reality, it was a mental stronghold based on the lie of perfectionism. I would wait until there was no possible way for me to succeed to even think about starting projects, or if I did start them, I would procrastinate until I felt hopeless against the deadline.

Maybe you can relate. Maybe every relationship you enter ends up the same way—because you sabotage it by rejecting others before they can reject you. Maybe you have New Year's resolutions to lose weight or get fit or study and pray more, but when you miss one day you give up completely. The demonic cycle is called self-sabotage. The enemy does not have to launch a new attack in your life because the lie he planted years ago works for him.

If you want to break the power of demonic cycles in your life, you first have to recognize the pattern. You have to pay attention to your triggers—the devil knows how to get your goat—your outcomes and your feelings afterward. You have to decide to put an end to the pattern. When you decide to align your will with the Lord instead of the lie in your soul, you will break the cycle.

The apostle Paul offers some good advice:

> For though we walk in the flesh, we do not war according to the flesh. For the weapons of our warfare are not carnal but mighty in God for pulling down strongholds, casting down arguments and every high thing that exalts itself against the knowledge of God, bringing every thought into captivity to the obedience of Christ, and being ready to punish all disobedience when your obedience is fulfilled.
>
> 2 Corinthians 10:3–6 NKJV

Neglecting to cast down a vain imagination is what got you into this demonic pattern to begin with. Being vigilant to think about what you are thinking about, to take ungodly thoughts captive with the Word of God and to submit yourself to the Lord and resist the devil will free you from demonic patterns that have plagued you for months, years or even the majority of your life. You can choose not to be led by your flesh or your emotions. You can choose to be led by the Spirit and take authority over every other spirit that vies for your attention.

If you want to break demonic cycles in your life, humble yourself and ask the Holy Spirit to help you find the verses in Scripture that will serve as your double-edged sword to slice to pieces the demonic strongholds in your mind. Whether it is a generational curse or you need full-blown deliverance, the blood of Jesus, the name of Christ and the Word of God are more powerful weapons than anything Satan has in his arsenal.

Dig down to the root of your thinking. Where did it start? Forgive anyone who hurt you. Forgive yourself. Receive forgiveness from the Lord for your wrong thinking and self-sabotage. Ask the Lord to fill you with His Holy Spirit, love the people around you, take on a new attitude and call those things that are not as though they were. As you do, you will begin to see things as He does—through the eyes of faith—and your behavior will begin to change. You will break the demonic cycle and stop walking in vicious circles. I assure you, whom the Son sets free is free indeed (see John 8:36).

A Revival of Holiness

> I continue to dream and pray about a revival of holiness in our day that moves forth in mission and creates authentic community in which each person can be unleashed through the empowerment of the Spirit to fulfill God's creational intentions.[5]

Those were the words of John Wesley, co-founder of Methodism. In 1982, David Wilkerson prophesied of this coming revival of holiness.

> I believe that even now my pen is anointed by the Spirit of God when I tell you that He is going to sovereignly move upon His church and awaken it anew to Bible holiness. The chosen of God are going [to] be stirred in their inner man; the Spirit is going to convict and tug and pull—until believers are once

again yearning for spiritual cleansing and deliverance from the power of sin.

Backslidden, cold-hearted church goers are going to be shaken and convicted by the powerful probings of the Holy Spirit. Judgment will begin in the house of God, and the Lord's holiness will be revealed in the inner man. Secret sin is going to be exposed, everywhere, and many, many Christians are going to be convicted and warned by God to lay their sin down, forsake it, or be judged openly, severely.

Lukewarm, backslidden ministers are going to see the standard of holiness raised in the land, and they will either turn to the Lord with fasting and praying, with tears and godly sorrow, and repentance—or, they will resist and be confirmed in their deadness and unconcern. But I believe every true minister of Christ who longs for restoration of Purity in the church, will experience a new call to diligent prayer and a renewed hatred for private and national sins.

We are going to see old-fashioned Holy Ghost conviction falling upon both sinners and Christians in churches all over this nation. I take that to be a Holy Ghost fact. It's already beginning to happen. In few months we received letters and phone calls from various ministers throughout the country telling of the sovereign moving of God's Spirit in their churches, with entire congregations completely shaken by powerful conviction of the Holy Spirit. Ministers report a renewed emphasis in their preaching against sin and compromise in their churches. They tell of people running to altars and repenting, crying out to God for a new baptism of love and cleansing in their souls. Covetousness, bitterness, and worldlimindedness are being confessed and forsaken. Their people are beginning to turn from wicked ways, and there is now a returning to the old paths of righteousness, by faith. Without being forced, they are beginning to fast and pray for a new vision of mercy and grace.[6]

Let it be so, Lord! My friend Becca Greenwood, co-founder of Christian Harvest International and author of *Authority to*

Tread, sees this day drawing closer. As she looks at the condition of the world around us and even the conditions of many in the Church, she clearly sees that we are in desperate need of a true embracing of His holiness. I am sure you would agree. How much more so for prophets and prophetic people who claim to speak for God? Listen to her words and get into agreement:

> I also firmly believe that God is calling for a sold-out holiness movement birthed from spiritual holiness and glory encounters with Him. When we encounter His light, truth, magnificent holiness and fire He captivates our minds and hearts. Not only are we to walk a lifestyle of holiness because we determine to do so, but the more we encounter Him; the more we encounter His unending magnificence and holiness; the more we encounter His love; the more we encounter the infilling of the Holy Spirit and His fire and truth; we become ones who desire to walk pure without compromise because of His sacrifice on the cross, resurrection life, His immense love and great holiness. The truth is once we encounter Him, we know that we know Him and we just cannot be the same. His fire and passion should ignite a consuming fire and passion within each of us.[7]

Here are three voices from three different generations in the body of Christ all calling for a holiness movement. Make it four. I see the same thing. As I said before, I believe that a key to a Third Great Awakening is humble, holy prophets who will point God's people toward repentance.

Next-Level Prophetic Exercises

Pursuing holiness is a lifelong quest. The tempter will always look for a place in you that is not purified. Jezebel will always look for your price. Cultivating holiness and purity will insulate you from these attacks, but many times deliverance ministry is required to deal with ungodly roots that cause you to pursue sinful desires. Engage in these prophetic exercises to help you root out anything that hinders holiness.

- ✓ Understand what true holiness is and embrace the command to be holy, knowing that it is a cooperative effort between your will and the Holy Spirit's power in your life.
- ✓ Pray for a revelation of the power of holiness in your heart as it relates to releasing a pure prophetic flow. The two go hand in hand.
- ✓ Pray that you would hunger and thirst after righteousness, which is connected to His holiness, and that anything unholy would be distasteful to you.
- ✓ Be willing to allow the Holy Spirit to convict you in areas of unholiness and repent.
- ✓ Ask the Lord to help you see patterns of sin that are rooted in demonic cycles or oppressive demonic strongholds that need to be broken, and then break them with His help, possibly through the help of a qualified deliverance ministry.

In the next chapter we go deep into the realm of faithfulness. Without faithfulness, the enemy can tempt us in many ways to misuse our prophetic gift or exploit it for ungodly purposes.

10

Faithfulness: The Prophet's Servitude

From Jesus Christ, who is the faithful witness.

Revelation 1:5

We prophecy by an unction of the Holy Spirit—not out of our soul, out of our gifting or out of the idolatry in someone's heart—and we would do well to remember that Jesus Christ is the faithful witness. What is more, one fruit of the Spirit is faithfulness (Galatians 5:22 NKJV). If you want to get to the next level of your prophetic gifting, practicing faithfulness—and exercising all the fruits of the Spirit for that matter—is baseline. We need to be faithful to the Lord, faithful to our families, faithful to our ministries, faithful to those God has called us to walk with and faithful to express our prophetic giftings only if, always, when and how He tells us.

God called the prophet Moses "faithful in all My house" (Numbers 12:7 NKJV). Scripture describes the prophet Daniel as faithful (see Daniel 6:4). David was faithful to Saul even when the king was trying to kill him (see 1 Samuel 26). The Holy Spirit purposely recorded the faithfulness of these and other prophets, like Isaiah, Jeremiah, Ezekiel.

In fact, faithfulness to God's plan is one of the things that sets apart true prophets from false prophets. False prophets are not faithful followers of God's Spirit (see Ezekiel 13:3). They are not faithful followers of God's Word (see Ezekiel 13:7). False prophets have dull prophetic edges that put those who hear their words in harm's way. The Lord spoke to Jeremiah about false prophets:

> Then the LORD said to me: The prophets prophesy lies in My name. I have not sent them nor have I commanded them nor have I spoken to them. They prophesy to you a false vision and divination, and emptiness, and the deceit of their heart.
>
> Jeremiah 14:14

I do not believe most false prophets start out as false prophets. While some prophets are self-proclaimed and therefore not true prophets to begin with, I believe true prophets can enter into a deception that puts them on a path to false prophethood and causes them to deceive others. Paul warned Timothy that in the last days "evil men and seducers will grow worse and worse, deceiving and being deceived" (2 Timothy 3:13). False prophets fall into that category of evil men (and women) who bring "swift destruction upon themselves" (2 Peter 2:1). Faithful prophets deliver prophetic words that are sharper than any two-edged sword.

Whether you are a prophet, a prophetic intercessor or a believer who prophesies at the unction of the Holy Spirit, there are rewards for faithfulness. Proverbs 28:20 declares that "a faithful man will abound with blessings." Psalm 31:23 promises the Lord will preserve the faithful. And Jesus commended the good and faithful servant (see Matthew 25:21, 23).

Depending on which translation you use, you can find the word *faithful* more than 75 times in Scripture. Entire books have been written on faithfulness, so I will not do an exhaustive study here. Let's look at a few Hebrew and Greek words describing faithfulness so you can get a clearer understanding of what it means to God. *Bible Study Tools*'s King James Version Old Testament Hebrew Lexicon tells us the Hebrew word *emuwnah* in Proverbs 28:20 translates as "firmness, fidelity, steadfastness, steadiness." The Hebrew word *aman* in Psalm 31:23 means "to support, confirm, be faithful." Finally, the King James Version New Testament Greek Lexicon tells us that the Greek word *pistos* in Matthew 25:21 and verse 23 translates as "trusty, faithful" and is used to describe people "who show themselves faithful in the transaction of business, the execution of commands, or the discharge of official duties." It refers to "one who has kept his plighted faith" and is "worthy of trust" and "can be relied" upon.

Faithfulness is a prerequisite for authentic prophets. Apostle John Eckhardt said this in his book *Prophet, Arise!*:

> Prophets look for the faithful. Prophets love faithfulness. Prophets love the faithful. The faithful are those who are steadfast with God. The faithful are the ones who serve God without compromise. Prophets grieve when there is no faithfulness.
>
> Prophets encourage the faithful. They remind the faithful of God's blessings and faithfulness to them. They encourage the faithful to keep moving ahead in spite of any obstacles and persecutions. Prophets will preach faithfulness.[1]

I might add that prophets need to be examples of faithfulness. There is a certain statesmanship required to carry the prophetic mantle. That statesmanship is rooted in faithfulness to God's true words, whether Scripture or prophetic utterances, dreams and visions.

Faithfulness is the baseline of prophetic ministry. Faithful prophets have an affection for God that supersedes affection for the world. They firmly hold to their duties and tightly buckle the belt of truth so that their prophetic edge can slice through anything that opposes the will of God. If you want to get to the next level in the prophetic, be faithful, because God knows that "he who is faithful in what is least is faithful also in much. And he who is dishonest in the least is dishonest also in much" (Luke 16:10).

Remember the Scripture promise that comes after "well done, you good and faithful servant": "You have been faithful over a few things. I will make you ruler over many things. Enter the joy of your master" (Matthew 25:23). We know that Elisha was faithful to Elijah in little things, even pouring water over his hands. When Elijah was taken up, Elisha received a double portion of his anointing and did even more miracles. We need to be faithful where God has planted us and not get so antsy to get to the next level that we try to bust down the doors on our own.

We need mentoring and feedback from apostles and prophets who have traveled a little farther down the road. And we need to serve them. Many were trained for prophetic ministry through serving Samuel (see 1 Samuel 19:19–24). This biblical principle still holds true today. Faithful service brings promotion. Do not run from your Samuel. Be faithful.

Elijah's Other Servant

Picture this. Elijah was running for his life from the wicked queen Jezebel. His servant was supposed to protect him. Instead, he stayed behind in Beersheba. Elijah could have used some support. He did not need to be isolated in the wilderness with his fearful imaginations of Jezebel's henchman catching up with him. But there is no indication that Elijah's servant even so much as tried to stand by his side.

That has always puzzled me. Elijah's servant had just watched God bring rain to the land at Elijah's word after a long drought.

Elijah's servant had just witnessed Elijah call down fire from heaven. Elijah's servant had witnessed his man of God defeat 850 prophets with his sword. God only knows how many other miracles Elijah's servant witnessed. Yet at the first sign of trouble, Elijah's servant failed to discern his need and stayed behind in Beersheba, a fertile land of plenty, while Elijah isolated himself in the wilderness.

Well, Elijah's servant missed out. That is the last we hear of him. He could have been in line for a double portion anointing, but he forfeited it by not sticking with Elijah through thick and thin. God gave Elijah a new servant not too long after this. God gave him Elisha to carry on his ministry. In contrast to Elijah's first servant, Elisha refused to leave his side. Elijah even commanded him twice to stay behind, and Elisha refused to leave him.

From the beginning, you can see Elisha's fervent spirit for the Lord. Elisha was plowing with twelve yoke of oxen when Elijah passed by him and cast his mantle upon him. Let's listen in to the chronicle:

> And he left the oxen, and ran after Elijah, and said, Let me, I pray thee, kiss my father and my mother, and then I will follow thee. And he said unto him, Go back again: for what have I done to thee?
>
> And he returned back from him, and took a yoke of oxen, and slew them, and boiled their flesh with the instruments of the oxen, and gave unto the people, and they did eat. Then he arose, and went after Elijah, and ministered unto him.
>
> 1 Kings 19:20–21 KJV

Elisha served Elijah faithfully—and fervently. He was widely known in the kingdom of Israel as the one who poured water over Elijah's hands (2 Kings 3:11). Through his faithful, fervent service to Elijah, Elisha was actually serving God's purposes in the earth and being prepared to do even greater works than Elijah.

Elijah gave his apprentice three chances to leave his service. Would Elisha stick with him or rush out to launch his own ministry before God's perfect timing? Would Elisha hang tough with Elijah no matter where he went or what he did? Or would he take any excuse to bail out when the warfare got intense, like Elijah's other servant did when Jezebel came calling?

Elisha may or may not have known it, but Elijah was about to give him a great responsibility—as his successor. Elisha had already been anointed as his successor, but now it was nearing time to take the mantle of responsibility and carry on where Elijah would leave off. Let's look at Elisha's trio of tests:

> Just before GOD took Elijah to heaven in a whirlwind, Elijah and Elisha were on a walk out of Gilgal. Elijah said to Elisha, "Stay here. GOD has sent me on an errand to Bethel."
>
> Elisha said, "Not on your life! I'm not letting you out of my sight!" So they both went to Bethel.
>
> The guild of prophets at Bethel met Elisha and said, "Did you know that GOD is going to take your master away from you today?"
>
> "Yes," he said, "I know it. But keep it quiet."
>
> Then Elijah said to Elisha, "Stay here. GOD has sent me on an errand to Jericho."
>
> Elisha said, "Not on your life! I'm not letting you out of my sight!" So they both went to Jericho.
>
> The guild of prophets at Jericho came to Elisha and said, "Did you know that GOD is going to take your master away from you today?"
>
> "Yes," he said, "I know it. But keep it quiet."
>
> Then Elijah said to Elisha, "Stay here. GOD has sent me on an errand to the Jordan."
>
> Elisha said, "Not on your life! I'm not letting you out of my sight!" And so the two of them went their way together.
>
> 2 Kings 2:1–6 MESSAGE

Elisha knew his master was about to go up to heaven. Instead of bailing on him, he stuck closely by Elijah's side to draw everything he could from him.

> And it came to pass, when they were gone over, that Elijah said unto Elisha, Ask what I shall do for thee, before I be taken away from thee. And Elisha said, I pray thee, let a double portion of thy spirit be upon me. And he said, Thou hast asked a hard thing: nevertheless, if thou see me when I am taken from thee, it shall be so unto thee; but if not, it shall not be so.
>
> 2 Kings 2:9–10 KJV

Elisha was bold enough to ask Elijah for a double portion of his anointing before he went on to be with the Lord. He knew he would need it to continue the work of the ministry. Based on his service up to that time, Elijah was willing to entertain the request. It reminds me of when Jesus asked Peter, "Do you love me?" three times. Jesus was giving Peter more responsibility for the church in that process, just as Elijah was preparing Elisha for his own calling as prophet.

But would Elisha stick by his side until the end? Elisha would have to if he wanted that double portion.

> And it came to pass, as they still went on, and talked . . .
>
> 2 Kings 2:11 KJV

I like that. They walked on together and they talked. Can you imagine what they were talking about? Both men knew that their time together was limited. This was Elisha's last chance to draw wisdom from his mentor. It was Elijah's last chance to offer his spiritual son instruction.

While they were talking a chariot of fire parted them, and Elijah went up by a whirlwind into the heavens. Elisha saw it. Elisha received the double portion anointing for which he petitioned.

And here is my point: Elijah's other servant, the one who

stayed behind at Beersheba, was a candidate for this double portion anointing. At the very least, he was in line to receive a mighty impartation from Elijah. But Elijah's other servant was not willing to go with him through the hard times, to the hard places, with the hard words. Elijah's other servant did not have a fervent spirit for serving the Lord, so Elijah's other servant disappears into Bible obscurity, without even so much as a name by which to call him. But the Bible says Elisha went on to do twice as many miracles as his mentor. Elisha maintained his fervency until the end. Elisha was so fervent in spirit that the miraculous followed him after he was dead and buried.

> And it came to pass, as they were burying a man, that, behold, they spied a band of men; and they cast the man into the sepulchre of Elisha: and when the man was let down, and touched the bones of Elisha, he revived, and stood up on his feet.
>
> 2 Kings 13:21 KJV

Cultivating Faithfulness

Although faithfulness is a fruit of the Spirit, we still have to do our part to cultivate its growth in our heart. Put another way, we have to break up the fallow ground in our hearts that would prevent faithfulness—or any other fruit of the Spirit—from thriving in our souls. We have to cultivate the fruit of faithfulness. This is scriptural. Psalm 37:3 (NASB) tells us to "trust in the LORD and do good; Dwell in the land and cultivate faithfulness."

The question, then, is this: How do you cultivate faithfulness and thereby sharpen your prophetic edge? The answer can be found in one Merriam-Webster definition of *cultivate*: "to improve by labor, care, or study." This is a strategic pattern for cultivating the fruit of faithfulness in our hearts.

Let's start with labor. We are called to be faithful in prayer, but we can turn that around and pray for faithfulness. Remember, apart from Christ we "can do nothing" (John 15:5), but in Him we "can do all things" (Philippians 4:13). We can pray for God to root out any unfaithfulness, carelessness, unreliability, untrustworthiness, irresponsibility, negligence, irresolution, disobedience, disloyalty, dishonesty and unstable ways from our souls. Our flesh will always be hostile to God, but we can choose to labor in prayer and cooperate with the grace of God to work out any issues—from hurts and wounds to self-ambition—that cause us not to be fully faithful.

We need to take great care to be faithful, and that means waiting on God's leading before making commitments, understanding His perfect will and being quick to listen and slow to speak. Our yes needs to be yes, and our no needs to be no (see Matthew 5:37). Paul warned us to look carefully at how we walk (see Ephesians 5:15), and we should also be careful whom we walk with. Ultimately, we need to walk close to the Lord. We need to take great care to practice the presence of God. Consider the words of Christ:

> Remain in Me, as I also remain in you. As the branch cannot bear fruit by itself, unless it remains in the vine, neither can you, unless you remain in Me. I am the vine, you are the branches. He who remains in Me, and I in him, bears much fruit. For without Me you can do nothing.
>
> John 15:4–5

If prophets abide in the prototype Prophet, Jesus, faithfulness will not be an issue. Cultivating this fruit of the Spirit will be a byproduct of being careful to abide in Him and shun those things that try to seduce our hearts. The Father is glorified when we bear fruit—and fruit that remains (see John 15:16).

Finally, our study of the Word will cultivate faithfulness in our hearts. Faithfulness is rooted in trusting the Lord. Trusting the Lord requires faith. "Faith comes by hearing" the Word of God (Romans 10:17). Staying connected to the written Word of God, the Bible, is a lifeline and a plumb line for prophets and prophetic people. Prophets flow in revelation gifts—words of wisdom, words of knowledge, discerning of spirits, gift of prophecy—and can get out of balance with the *rhema* word of God if they are not rooted in the written Word of God. Feeding on the Word of God builds up your spirit man, which cultivates faithfulness to God.

Next-Level Prophetic Exercises

Aren't you glad God is faithful to you? He "is not a man, that He should lie" (Numbers 23:19). His promises are yes and amen (see 2 Corinthians 1:20). He will never leave you or forsake you (see Deuteronomy 31:6). Getting to the next level in the prophetic demands ever-increasing faithfulness.

✓ Meditate on Jesus Christ, the Prophet, as a faithful witness. He only did what He saw the Father do (see John 5:19). We should only say what we see or hear the Lord do, thereby exercising our gift faithfully.

✓ Meditate on the many verses I shared in this chapter on faithfulness. Let the Holy Spirit convict you if you are falling short. Ask Him for the grace to rise up higher in faithfulness.

✓ Who are you faithfully serving? As outlined in this chapter, a principle in Scripture is serving other people faithfully as unto the Lord before being released into the next level of your gifting.

✓ Ask the Holy Spirit to help you cultivate His fruit of faithfulness in your life.

In the next chapter we will take a hard and honest look at apostolic accountability. If you have walked through spiritual abuse, you may feel tempted to skip this chapter. Do not. It could be the key to going to the next level in your prophetic ministry.

11

Apostolic Accountability: The Prophet's Safeguard

Accountability is vital to sharpening your prophetic edge and cutting through to the next level. I will say that again: Accountability is vital to sharpening your prophetic edge and cutting through to the next level. It is not enough to be accountable to God. In this hour of Church history God is not raising up Lone Ranger prophets but companies of prophets who run together and work with other fivefold gifts. We need to align with others who will hold us accountable for not only our prophetic utterances but also our general character. This is a safety net.

I understand all too well that accountability is a sensitive subject for many believers because of spiritual abuse in the church. Indeed, I understand spiritual abuse all too well because I was a victim of it early in my prophetic ministry. But that does not justify a negative attitude toward godly accountability. David was a victim of spiritual abuse in its most extreme form. King Saul used, abused and sorely persecuted David almost to the point of death, but that did not stop David from submitting himself to the prophet Nathan after he committed adultery with Bathsheba.

Every prophet—green or veteran—must take responsibility for his or her actions. No prophet is perfect. Even the most seasoned prophet can miss it from time to time. It goes back to humility. Mature prophets will humbly admit their error and seek the Lord's face for revelation on how they erred. Proud, Lone Ranger prophets will move on to the next city on their itinerary without considering—or taking responsibility for—the damage they caused. Hear me: If we buck and fight against accountability, then it only shows our lack of maturity and readiness for public ministry.

Apostolic Accountability

Prophets are undoubtedly vital to the end time Church. Apostles recognize this truth and welcome prophets to work alongside them to build the Church and to equip believers for the work of the ministry. The restoration of apostolic ministry and the accountability apostles provide for prophets does not hinder prophetic people. Rather, it acts as a safety net, as there is safety in submission.

What if Jonah had apostolic accountability? Maybe he would not have wound up under a tree with a bad attitude, wishing he was dead. Like Jonah, New Testament prophets who start off walking in God's will but take a detour are apt to fall. True apostles are spiritual fathers and mothers with the prophets' best interests at heart. Remember what the apostle Paul said to the church at Corinth:

> I'm writing as a father to you, my children. I love you and want you to grow up well, not spoiled. There are a lot of people around who can't wait to tell you what you've done wrong, but there aren't many fathers willing to take the time and effort to help you grow up.

> 1 Corinthians 4:14–15 MESSAGE

The purpose of Paul's bold words to the Corinthians is repeated here: "Therefore I write these things being absent, lest being present I should use sharpness, according to the power which the Lord hath given me to edification, and not to destruction" (2 Corinthians 13:10 KJV).

By speaking the truth in love, however uncomfortable it may be to receive, apostolic fathers and mothers are helping to protect New Testament prophets from spirits like Jezebel and witchcraft. An apostolic covering and some fatherly correction may have saved Jonah's ministry, but the last we read of him he was sitting outside Nineveh wishing he was dead.

I launched the Ignite prophetic network with its many divisions because it is difficult for people to find true, healthy apostolic accountability. At some level, accountability is accountability, but I believe aligning with apostolic authority offers the surest safety net.

That said, I want to take a moment to address the realm of apostolic and prophetic authority. Some camps within the Body of Christ have carried apostolic authority to the extreme, while others refuse to accept it. The safest approach is to see how the New Testament apostles used their authority. The common denominator is edification. Consider the words of Paul the apostle:

> I may seem to be boasting too much about the authority given to us by the Lord. But our authority builds you up; it doesn't tear you down. So I will not be ashamed of using my authority. I'm not trying to frighten you by my letters.
>
> 2 Corinthians 10:8–10 NLT

When Paul brought correction to the Corinthians, he was not trying to tear them apart. He was speaking the truth in love. He was trying to build them up in the faith of Christ. He was not trying to frighten them with his strong language. He was trying to stir them to repentance and a reverential fear of the Lord. That is true apostolic authority.

Apostles recognize and welcome prophets to work alongside them to build the Church and to equip believers for ministry (see Ephesians 4:11–12). Where other ministry offices have been threatened by or have misunderstood the prophet's gift, healthy apostles embrace grace and seek to build a platform for the prophetic voice. That platform, however, is only accessible to stable prophets who are willing to be held accountable for their utterances.

Consider Nehemiah. Nehemiah was a type of apostle who was called to rebuild the walls of Jerusalem. Who was working alongside Nehemiah? The trumpeters, who were types of prophets. The trumpeters were submitted to Nehemiah's vision to rebuild the wall and his authority to oversee the completion of that vision. The Old Testament apostolic builder, in turn, welcomed and depended upon the prophetic watchmen to warn him if the enemies were approaching (see Nehemiah 4:18).

So the apostle and prophets worked together in a dangerous situation, as several hostile forces sought to kill them in order to stop the work. What would have happened to the trumpeters if they had abandoned Nehemiah's apostolic covering to follow self-will instead of God's will? They may have fallen prey to the Arabs, the Ammonites or the Ashdodites (types of demonic guards) who opposed the building.

Likewise, New Testament prophets who start off walking in God's will but take a detour into rebellion, stubbornness, pride, lust or any other sinful lifestyle are apt to fall prey to demonic guards who oppose the building of the glorious Church of Jesus Christ.

A True Spiritual Father

A young man I will refer to as Bill once told me the story of how his apostle put such a demand on him to perform in service of the ministry that it caused him problems on the home front.

His kids were unruly and resentful. His taxes were overdue. He never had time to visit his parents. The pressure to perform became so great that eventually, despite his best efforts, he could not keep up, and he fell down on his volunteer ministry duties (which exceeded thirty hours a week).

The apostle put him on notice that he would be "sat down" if he did not straighten up, so Bill worked harder. The apostle told him he would be keeping a close eye on him. Well, Bill rose to the occasion and performed at a high level in the ministry, though his family life and work continued to suffer. The apostle's response? "Congratulations. I didn't think you could do it. But you proved me wrong."

That is not the heart of a true apostle. Even with all the problems in the Corinthian church—and there were many, including divisions, carnality, immorality, fornication, abusing the Lord's Supper, a lack of love, disorder and wrong teachings about the resurrection of the dead—the apostle Paul said this: "I have the highest confidence in you, and I take great pride in you. You have greatly encouraged me and made me happy despite all our troubles" (2 Corinthians 7:4 NLT). That is the heart of a true spiritual father.

So what does a true spiritual father look like? I mentioned a few characteristics earlier in this chapter. But let's look at how Scripture bears it out—not with mere descriptive buzzwords but in clear-cut actions that demonstrate how spiritual fathers responded to their spiritual children.

Paul's heartfelt care and concern for his spiritual sons leaps from the pages of his epistles. True spiritual fathers and mothers have true relationships with their spiritual children, and those relationships are rooted in the love of Christ.

Paul trained Timothy, not to forward Paul's ministry but to forward the Kingdom. He repeatedly spoke "grace, mercy, and peace" over Timothy's life, despite his flaws (1 Timothy 1:2; 2 Timothy 1:2). Paul encouraged Timothy when he was afraid (2 Timothy 1:7). He shared his heart and his wisdom with Timothy so he could be a more effective minister of the Gospel (see the book of 2 Timothy). He even cared about Timothy's stomach problems (1 Timothy 5:23). Paul prayed for Timothy constantly, rather than just demanding Timothy's service to him (2 Timothy 1:3–7). He was grateful to have Timothy in his life, and he treated Timothy with respect.

Consider the spiritual dynamic between Paul and Timothy:

> Every time I say your name in prayer—which is practically all the time—I thank God for you, the God I worship with my whole life in the tradition of my ancestors. I miss you a lot, especially when I remember that last tearful good-bye, and I look forward to a joy-packed reunion.
>
> 2 Timothy 1:3–4 MESSAGE

Once again, spiritual mentoring demands relationship. You cannot rent a spiritual father. True spiritual accountability, which is vital in this hour, comes out of true, balanced, healthy relationships where the spiritual mentors have the best interests of their spiritual mentees at heart, even if that means releasing them into what God has for them next. This is a true spiritual father.

A spiritual father loves at all times. When correction must come, it comes out of a spirit of love rather than a spirit of fear, control, intimidation, manipulation or condemnation. Remember, it was Paul, a strong model of a spiritual father, who was used by the Holy Spirit to offer us a revelation of what love in action looks like. Although everyone has bad days and goes through trials, 1 Corinthians 13:4–7 (NLT) reveals how those who deem themselves spiritual fathers, mothers and mentors should behave toward those under their care:

> Love is patient and kind. Love is not jealous or boastful or proud or rude. It does not demand its own way. It is not irritable, and it

keeps no record of being wronged. It does not rejoice about injustice but rejoices whenever the truth wins out. Love never gives up, never loses faith, is always hopeful, and endures through every circumstance.

Iron Sharpens Iron

My friend apostle Clay Nash, founder of The CityGate in Southaven, Mississippi, talks about accountability in his book *Relational Authority*. In it, he explains that authentic authority is relational; it works through relationship to influence people:

> Without relationship, I will not willingly accept someone's authority, and so, they cannot influence me. The quality of relationship I have with another determines how much they can influence me. Through relationship, their authority can influence me only as far as our shared trust, knowledge, and experience. For example, my wife can influence me at a deep level; my friends can influence me at a moderate level, and my neighbors can influence me at a light level. Because I am in a different relationship will all three people groups, their authority in my life is different and consequently, they influence me differently.[1]

Living the Christian life is a journey toward maturity in Christ. That is why Jesus gave His Church a handful of equipping gifts. But the practical aspect of being trained as a skilled servant who moves in rhythm with Christian brothers and sisters (and husbands, wives, daughters and sons) is not always a textbook experience.

Let's get real for a moment. Silly putty does not sharpen iron. Plastic does not sharpen iron. Not even sandpaper sharpens iron, although at times you may feel like a fellow believer is aggressively rubbing your soul with sandpaper. No, Solomon in his wisdom tells us that it takes iron to sharpen iron: "Iron sharpens iron, so one man sharpens another" (Proverbs 27:17

NASB). That implies pressure, abrasion, pressure, abrasion, pressure, abrasion and so on until the knife is sharp.

You may be saying, "I don't need to be the sharpest knife in the drawer." Consider the alternative. Any five-star chef, or even a first-year fry cook, will testify to the fact that a knife is useless if it is not sharp. A sharp knife can cut a vine-ripe tomato into thin slices suitable for gourmet salads. A dull knife, on the other hand, will simply crush the tomato and ruin your recipe.

The good news is that apostolic metal is as hard as it comes. The bad news is that apostolic metal is as hard as it comes. We need to be spiritually sharp with metallic souls set on God's purposes in order to live the apostolic life successfully. It takes a special breed and a heavy supply of God's grace to carry the cross over the finish line. Apostolic metal is hard enough to endure the persecution and subsequent suffering that comes with persisting in God's will.

Any good butcher will tell you that the harder the metal, the longer it will hold its edge. By the same token, the harder the metal of which the knife is made, the harder it is to sharpen. The sharpener has to be made of a material that is harder than the metal in order to grind down the hundreds of tiny saw-like teeth that get twisted and bent out of alignment through repeated use. Butchers and professional cooks give their knives a few strokes on the sharpener before each use.

Indeed, sharpening is a constant process, especially in the apostolic life rife with spiritual warfare. We need iron-like strength that will break, pulverize and bust up the kingdom of darkness. We need an iron-like will to continue to pursue God's will in the face of resistance from principalities and powers. But even with hard-as-steel spiritual traits, our souls can become weary in the day-to-day battle that is not merely against principalities and powers but also against flesh—ours and others' (read: strong-willed children, cranky bosses and nagging spouses). You can respond in one of two ways during the sharpening process. You can moan, groan, whine, complain, cry, pout and pity yourself and extend your pain, or you can yield to the iron furnace of suffering and emerge as sparkling gold (Isaiah 48:10).

Remember, blacksmiths have to put iron into fire to make it malleable before removing it and shaping it with quick, repeated blows with a hammer. Who is the blacksmith in your life? Jesus often uses those closest to us as tools to show us the muck and mire in our souls that is hindering our success. But instead of becoming offended, angry and unforgiving, apostolic living requires us to praise the Lord in the midst of the admittedly often unpleasant sharpening process. Do you have an ax to grind? Humbly iron out your differences with brothers and sisters and watch God work.

Obeying His Word will put that much-needed iron into our souls and take us one step closer to conforming to His image. The psalmist said, "Invigorate my soul so I can praise you well, use your decrees to put iron in my soul" (Psalm 119:175 MESSAGE). If you allow the Word of God to change (sharpen) you, then before you know it the overbearing attitude of your sister-in-law or the pushy demeanor of your brother in the faith will not even bother you, and you can concentrate on fighting the real enemy.

The Word of God is surely sharper than any surgeon's scalpel and cuts the enemy to bits every time when you swing that sword in faith. Remember the Lord's promise through the prophet Isaiah to those who trust in Him:

> Behold, I will make you to be a new, sharp, threshing instrument which has teeth; you shall thresh the mountains and beat them small, and shall make the hills like chaff. You shall winnow them, and the wind shall carry them away, and the tempest or whirlwind shall scatter them. And you shall rejoice in the Lord, you shall glory in the Holy One of Israel.
>
> Isaiah 41:15–16 AMPC

Next-Level Prophetic Exercises

Accountability has become a dirty word for many believers in the Body of Christ due to authoritarian leadership styles and controlling ministries. But the Bible speaks over and again about submission to authority. Prophets need apostolic accountability.

✓ Are you resistant to apostolic accountability? Ask the Lord to show you the root of this resistance if you do not already know what it is.

✓ When you discover the root of your resistance to apostolic accountability, ask the Lord to sever the root. That may mean healing or deliverance. It may just be an attitude adjustment. It almost always means forgiving someone who misused their authority in your life, including parents, pastors, a schoolteacher or police officers.

✓ Examine your current alignments. Is the leadership toxic and controlling? It may be time to find a new covering that will celebrate rather than persecute you when God promotes you.

✓ Study verses on submission to authority to renew your mind in this area. Here are a few: Hebrews 13:17; Romans 13:1–7 and 1 Peter 5:5.

Are you ready to become that threshing instrument about which Isaiah prophesied? Are you ready to go to the next level? Submit yourself to the sharpening process at the hands of your fivefold ministers, friends, foes and family—and, of course, the Spirit of God—and emerge from the iron furnace as a razor-sharp battle-ax fit to cut through any spiritual opposition. From major trials and tribulations to life's everyday struggles, your fire-tested, apostolic metal will lead you into victorious living.

Conclusion

New Level, New Devil

You have probably heard it said, "New level, new devil." I do not know who said it first—some attribute it to Joyce Meyer—but whoever said it first, it is totally scriptural. Paul told the church at Corinth, "For a great and effective door has opened to me, and there are many adversaries" (1 Corinthians 16:9).

But do not let that deter you.

There are many levels of the prophetic, so the sharpening process never ends—and there are many ways to sharpen your prophetic edge. You can be confident in this: "He who began a good work in you will perfect it" (Philippians 1:6).

We will continue returning to the potter's house at different times and seasons. But that is not a bad thing. Much revelation is given to prophets in the potter's house. The experience helps to keep pride from taking root in the prophet's life. Prophets with such strong revelatory gifts can have a tendency to become prideful and arrogant without occasional visits to the potter's house on the way to the next level.

So are you ready to go to the next level? Read this book more than once. At different phases in your life, you will need to hear these truths again.

Notes

Introduction

1. C. S. Lewis, *Mere Christianity* (New York: HarperCollins, 2001), 28.

Chapter 1: Your Prophetic Gifting

1. You can learn more about these aspects of prophetic ministry in my book *The Heart of the Prophetic: Keys to Flowing in a More Powerful Prophetic Anointing* (Jennifer LeClaire Ministries, 2007).

Chapter 2: The Making of a Prophet

1. I have an entire book on this subject called *The Making of a Prophet: Practical Advice for Developing Your Prophetic Voice* (Chosen Books, 2014) that I recommend.

Chapter 5: Humility: The Prophet's Equalizer

1. Matthew Henry, *Matthew Henry's Commentary on the Whole Bible: Volume VI–VIII, Titus–Revelation*, ed. Anthony Uyl (Woodstock, Ontario: Devoted Publishing, 2018), 140.

2. Mother Teresa, *The Joy in Loving*, comp. Jaya Chalika and Edward Le Joly (New York: Penguin, 2000), 406.

Chapter 6: Selflessness: The Prophet's Quest

1. R. Loren Sandford, *Purifying the Prophetic: Breaking Free from the Spirit of Self-Fulfillment* (Minneapolis: Chosen, 2005), 62.

Chapter 7: Prayer: The Prophet's Gateway

1. E. M. Bounds, *The Complete Works of E. M. Bounds on Prayer* (Grand Rapids: Baker, 1990), 287.

2. E. M. Bounds, *The Complete Works of E. M. Bounds on Prayer* (Grand Rapids: Baker, 1990), 347.

Chapter 8: Warfare: The Prophet's Mantra

1. Jennifer LeClaire, "One (Big) Hope," *Charisma*, November 1, 2012, https:// www.charismamag.com/spirit/evangelism-missions/15672-one-big-hope.

Chapter 9: Holiness: The Prophet's Cry

1. David Wilkerson, "Be Ye Holy," April 1, 1982, World Challenge, https:// worldchallenge.org/content/be-ye-holy.

2. Charles Spurgeon, "Receiving the Holy Ghost," July 13, 1884, *Metropolitan Tabernacle Pulpit Vol. 30*, The Spurgeon Center, https://www.spurgeon.org /resource-library/sermons/receiving-the-holy-ghost#flipbook/.

3. Charles Spurgeon, "The Sine Qua Non," April 16, 1870, *Metropolitan Tabernacle Pulpit Vol. 16*, The Spurgeon Center, https://www.spurgeon.org/resource -library/sermons/the-sine-qua-non#flipbook/.

4. Charles Spurgeon, "Holiness Demanded," Blue Letter Bible, https://www .blueletterbible.org/Comm/spurgeon_charles/sermons/2902.cfm.

5. John Wesley, quoted in Daniel Park, "Wesley's Dream for Evangelism and Mission," Chesterbrook United Methodist Church, April 30, 2017, https://www .chesterbrookchurch.org/wesleys-dream-for-evangelism-and-mission/.

6. David Wilkerson, "Coming Soon—A Revival of Holiness," February 1, 1982, World Challenge, https://worldchallenge.org/content/coming-soon-%E2%80%94 -revival-holiness.

7. Rebecca Greenwood, "Walking in Holiness," *Christian Harvest International*, April 15, 2014, http://79294.inspyred.com/apps/articles/web/articleid /80137/columnid/6916/default.asp.

Chapter 10: Faithfulness: The Prophet's Servitude

1. John Eckhardt, *Prophet, Arise!* (Lake Mary, Fla.: Charisma House, 2015), 111.

Chapter 11: Apostolic Accountability: The Prophet's Safeguard

1. Clay Nash, *Relational Authority* (Sharpsburg, Md.: Spring Mill Publishing, 2015), 72.

Jennifer LeClaire is a conference speaker, internationally recognized author and prophetic voice to her generation. She inspires and challenges believers to pursue intimacy with God, cultivate their spiritual gifts and walk in the fullness of what God has called them to do. Jennifer contends for awakening in the nations through intercession and spiritual warfare, strong apostolic preaching and practical prophetic teaching that equips the saints for the work of the ministry.

Jennifer is the senior leader of Awakening House of Prayer in Fort Lauderdale, Florida, founder of the Ignite Network and founder of the Awakening Blaze prayer movement.

Having served as the first-ever editor of *Charisma* magazine, she has written more than 25 books, including *The Making of a Prophet, The Spiritual Warrior's Guide to Defeating Jezebel, Satan's Deadly Trio, The Heart of the Prophetic, Mornings with the Holy Spirit, The Spiritual Warfare Battle Plan* and many others. Some of her work has been translated into Spanish and Korean, and some is archived in the Flower Pentecostal Heritage Museum.

Beyond frequent appearances on The Elijah List, Jennifer writes one of *Charisma*'s most popular blogs, *The Plumb Line*, and contributes often to *Charisma*'s *Prophetic Insight* blog. She has been interviewed on media outlets like *USA Today*, BBC, CBN, *Bill Martinez Live, Babbie's House, Atlanta Live*, Sid Roth's *It's Supernatural!* and more.

Jennifer is aligned with multiple ministries, including Chuck Pierce's apostolic network, Bishop Bill Hamon's Christian International, The Apostolic Council of Prophetic Elders (ACPE) led by Cindy Jacobs and The International Society of Deliverance Ministers (ISDM). She also sits on the media advisory board of the Hispanic Israel Leadership Coalition.

Jennifer has a testimony of God's power to set the captives free and claim beauty for ashes. She shares her story with women who need to understand the love and grace of God in a lost and dying world. Connect with her on Facebook, Twitter, YouTube and www.jenniferleclaire.org.